USING AND
MAINTAINING
CHURCH PROPERTY

CHURCH BUSINESS MANAGEMENT SERIES

USING AND MAINTAINING CHURCH PROPERTY

by Allen W. Graves

PRENTICE-HALL INC.,
Englewood Cliffs, New Jersey

Library of Congress Catalog Card Number: 65-24695

Printed in the United States of America

T 93928

PRENTICE-HALL INTERNATIONAL, INC., *London*
PRENTICE-HALL OF AUSTRALIA, PTY., LTD., *Sydney*
PRENTICE-HALL OF CANADA, LTD., *Toronto*
PRENTICE-HALL OF INDIA (PRIVATE) LTD., *New Delhi*
PRENTICE-HALL OF JAPAN, INC., *Tokyo*

To
Gaines S. Dobbins

EDITOR'S INTRODUCTION

THE PURPOSE of the series of books in which this volume is included is to provide new insight and specific guidance for managing effectively the affairs of churches and related non-profit organizations. These books represent the most comprehensive publishing project ever completed in the field of church management.

Each volume in this series is based on four major premises: First, if churches are to accomplish their distinctive purposes, their approaches to management must be at least as effective as those of other organizations. Second, some of the principles of management that are applied satisfactorily in business, government, hospitals, and elsewhere may be used appropriately and effectively in churches. Third, since churches are service-rendering rather than profit-making, and because of the uniqueness of their voluntary nature and trustee relationship, some of their management policies and practices must be different from those of commercial enterprises. Fourth, the differences between management approaches that are designed for secular organizations and management approaches that are relevant to the purposes of churches must be clearly identified and thoroughly understood.

These books are intended to (1) help clergy and laity develop additional competence for effective stewardship

of church management responsibilities, (2) provide stim-
ulation and practical suggestions for professional career
service as directors or ministers of management, and (3)
make available an educational basis for strengthening the
role of pastors as chief administrators of individual
churches.

In designing and preparing the material for this series
of books the editor and the authors were confronted with
basic questions to which answers had not been published.
What *is* church management? What is it *for?* What is it
not? What is it *not* for? What are its boundaries and its
components? The following formulation is a result of the
editor's pioneer effort to identify and delineate this field:

> *Church Management* is the science and art of adminis-
> tering church program development, financial resources,
> physical facilities, office services, staff personnel, and pro-
> gram promotion—according to effective standards of re-
> ligious stewardship. Included in this concept are such
> managerial processes as forecasting, planning, organizing,
> delegating, controlling, and reporting. Church manage-
> ment is a facilitating function and should be regarded not
> as an end in itself but as an important means to an end.

Many alert and imaginative congregations in recent
years have added to the employed staff a qualified career-
service director or minister of management. Usually he is
a person of considerable maturity, religious commitment,
management experience, and relevant training. He serves
as a professional consultant and resource leader in helping
church officers and staff, both volunteers and employees,
perform their administrative duties in relation to the ministry of:

1. *Program Development*—planning, organizing, and
   scheduling all appropriate means available to the
   church for accomplishing its objectives and goals.

2. *Financial Management*—obtaining, allocating, safe-guarding, disbursing, and accounting for all monetary resources.
3. *Property Management*—using, maintaining, and acquiring buildings and grounds, furniture, and equipment.
4. *Office Management*—providing systematic programs of scheduling, communicating, recording, and reporting designed to facilitate performance of other administrative functions.
5. *Personnel Management*—determining and describing staff positions; enlisting, assigning, and training staff personnel, both volunteers and employees; developing and maintaining staff morale.
6. *Program Promotion*—communicating the church's concept of its objectives, goals, accomplishments, potentialities, and needs.

Church management as viewed in this light, and when applied creatively through collaborative and democratic processes, may be regarded as a significant phase of a meaningful spiritual ministry. How effectively the author of each book in this series has amplified the foregoing philosophy may be determined by the readers themselves.

For invaluable advice and practical assistance throughout the planning and execution stages of this endeavor the editor is grateful to Dr. Nathan A. Baily, dean of the School of Business Administration, The American University. Dean Baily's keen interest and capable leadership stimulated the establishment of the Center for Church Business Management while facilitating the development of this series of books.

Clyde W. Humphrey
General Editor

Washington, D.C.

PREFACE

THE MANAGEMENT of church property is an important and increasingly complex task. Proper management means maximum use of church facilities. To make maximum use of new materials and equipment and to provide a well kept building at reasonable cost, it is important for the maintenance staff to be well informed. Additional training and information enable the maintenance staff to render more efficient service.

This book provides to church maintenance personnel, the property management committee, trustees, and others related to property management an understanding of many different facets of their work in readily available form. This volume can guide church officials in establishing proper administrative policies and in providing needed supervision to secure quality performance. Along with other books in this series it equips church leaders for effective, ethical, equitable, and economical church business management. This book should be particularly helpful to the church business administrator in training members of his staff.

Principles and practices in church business administration often differ from practices followed in business, industry, or government. The ultimate purpose of the church

10

is not to make a profit but to minister to the spiritual needs
of the people. This distinctive purpose affects the policies
and practices followed by a church in maintaining and
using its facilities.

"Maintenance" is used in this volume to include the operation of the buildings: heating, cooling, cleaning, repairing, and replacement needed to keep church property in
sound, usable, attractive, and comfortable condition. It
also includes the arrangement and protection of church
property. The term "church building" is used generically
to refer to any building used for religious purposes, including synagogue, temple, cathedral, or chapel. The term
"minister" or "pastor" is used to refer to the chief religious
leader of a particular congregation.

The book reflects the author's experience as pastor for
more than twenty years in churches large and small and,
since 1955, as Professor of Church Administration in the
Southern Baptist Theological Seminary where he serves
as Dean of the School of Religious Education.

The author records here his deep appreciation to those
who have shared information and evaluated the material
presented in this volume. He is deeply indebted to Mrs.
Watson Mills for the typing of the manuscript. The series
editor, the Reverend Clyde W. Humphrey made many
very helpful suggestions. Mr. Hugh G. E. Paull contrib-
uted the material in Chapter 15, "Questions for Review
and Discussion" and evaluated the manuscript from the
viewpoint of a church business manager. Mr. T. Robert
Allen, Jr., Superintendent of Buildings and Grounds, Southern Baptist Theological Seminary, Louisville, Kentucky,
supplied valuable technical information. To these and all
those faithful workmen with whom the author has worked
in churches and church-related institutions who have demonstrated good policies and practices in the use and maintenance of church property, sincere gratitude is expressed.

Allen W. Graves

CONTENTS

13

CONTENTS

Chapter 1

USING CHURCH PHYSICAL FACILITIES

A CHURCH needs a place to meet to carry on the activities necessary for achieving its objectives. In the first century A.D. churches owned no buildings; they secured their meeting places from others. When churches began to provide their own buildings the kinds of buildings were determined by the kinds of activities conducted in them. This book discusses appropriate uses of church property, and maintenance procedures for securing maximum use from all church facilities.

PRIORITY USE

Church buildings have a special significance that distinguishes them from public halls or commercial meeting places. They are set apart, specially dedicated to God for the specific purpose of worship, religious education, fellowship, and service. Priority in the use of church buildings should be given to those spiritual ministries of the church itself and to the community it serves through its witness and program.

Individuals and groups who traditionally use church buildings include church staff members, the worshipping congregation, church organiations, children in the nurs-

15

ery, the kindergarten or other weekday church school, wedding parties, funerals, and denominational agencies.

Some churches restrict the use of their facilities to their own membership. Others openly invite the use of their facilities by other groups in the community. Churches occasionally receive requests to use the organ and pianos for music instruction or practice. Use of recreation facilities is frequently requested by others. Before ruling in such instances, the church should carefully evaluate its own use of its facilities.

The church should evaluate community needs in the light of its own basic objectives before establishing regulations concerning the use of its facilities by outside groups. If the church is to conduct a social welfare ministry providing day care for children of working parents, clothing and food for underprivileged, and recreational activities or other group programs, then specific plans should be followed in providing facilities and using them properly.

USE OF SPACE

To maximize the use of church-owned facilities, an inventory should be made and a space-utilization chart prepared. Each room should have a number and a room assignment chart.

Some individuals and groups are thoughtless in their use of the building and its equipment. Accordingly, it is important to weigh the values received or given by making church facilities available to any and all groups.

Some congregations are quite willing to carry the pro rata cost of providing facilities for various civic groups. Others make a modest charge sufficient to pay for personnel services and for a proportionate part of the construction and maintenance costs. Yet other churches are so heavily programmed that they are unable to accommodate nonchurch groups.

RENTAL CONSIDERATIONS

In some communities, public or private school groups have rented, on a temporary or permanent basis, the education facilities of the church for weekday school use. This may occur in emergency situations where a fire or a student overload makes regular school facilities inadequate.

Similarly, when a church has some special need for space, as when rebuilding, remodeling, or relocating, it may rent space from a school, a fraternal organization, or a theater to provide emergency facilities. Such arrangements are temporary expedients since the church will normally need to have and use its own facilities. Whether temporary or long range, the arrangements should be stated in contractual form, specifying the areas involved, the rent to be paid, the maintenance services to be provided, the insurance coverages, and the procedures to be followed in replacing or repairing damaged equipment or buildings.

TAXATION ON RENTAL PROPERTY

In many communities any church-owned property not used for religious purposes is placed on the tax rolls. Taxable property may include that purchased for future expansion of the church. In many states this would include investment property purchased by or given to the church. Each congregation should carefully consider the legal, ethical, and moral issues involved in seeking or accepting tax exemption for income-producing property not being used directly for religious purposes.

Some churches face the question of whether to use portions of their buildings for a part of the week as income-producing areas and, at other times, for religious purposes. Such is especially true of religious education facilities used during the week for nonchurch-related school groups. Parking lots used by church members on Sunday are leased or rented for commercial operation at other times.

Some churches and many church-related agencies invest funds, usually endowment or trust funds, in the purchase or construction of business or industrial property which is then leased back to companies that prefer not to invest their capital in real estate. In many cases these properties are assessed in the normal procedure of taxation. In other cases the property is tax exempt because of its ownership by a religious organization.

TAX EXEMPTION OF CHURCH-OWNED PROPERTY

The propriety of church tax exemption as a part of the church and state relationship set forth in the United States' Constitution and its amendments, as well as the churches' own interpretations of the religious and ethical principles involved, has come under critical review in recent years. It is not the purpose of this book to resolve all questions regarding tax exemption for churches, but we have a rightful concern about the taxability of church-owned property that is used for income-producing purposes. Taxation of church-owned property is determined by state laws that vary widely among the states in both statement and interpretation. Generally, however, churches are tax exempt, either by the provisions of the state constitution or by statutes of state legislatures.

Tax Exemption of the Edifice: Exemption is provided by most states for the edifice of worship and the real estate upon which it stands, on the assumption that the power to tax is the power to control and ultimately to destroy.

The laws differ as to how much land is required for a church edifice. Some states limit the maximum valuation or acreage, or both, that may be exempted. If only a part of the church building is used for secular purposes— which in some states would be interpreted to include an apartment for the sexton or space for the operation of a parochial school—the building may be exempted in full, in part, or not at all. These matters should be thoroughly investigated before constructing buildings to be used wholly or in part by those not directly involved in the major functions of the church. The opportunity to exempt property from taxation is not an inalienable right; it is a privilege granted expressly either by the constitution or the legislature.

A lot on which a house of worship is under construction is usually not subject to taxation; but a vacant lot normally is. Property purchased for eventual church use ordinarily remains on the tax roll until actually used for religious purposes. A dwelling purchased for expansion of the church but rented until construction begins would normally stay on the tax rolls. If the building were removed and the land used for a parking area for church use exclusively, the property would qualify for exemption in most cases.

Three conditions must generally be met before tax exemption can be granted: (1) The property must be owned by a church, a religious society, or a religious denomination. Exemption is not allowable to the private owner of property rented or leased to a church. (2) The building(s) must definitely be dedicated to religious worship. (3) The acreage involved in tax exemption must be essential for the uses made by the church in its various programs. Excess acreage not used in church programs is generally denied exemption.

Tax authorities have been quite lenient in the use of church buildings for lectures, plays, and other nonchurch activities for which admission or rent is paid to the church by the group using the building. When such use is only occasional, questions are seldom raised about the nonprofit status of the church. Whenever a portion of a church building is rented out for a business or for any profit-making enterprise, however, that portion of the building is normally subject to taxation.

Tax Exemption of Parsonages: Twenty states have legislation exempting parsonages from taxation, and most of the other states actually do not assess taxes on church-owned parsonages. In some cases, the first $3,000 to $5,000 of assessed valuation is exempt. With the growth of church staffs, questions arise as to the number of church-owned residences that may be exempted.

The church business manager or the chairman of the finance committee should check annually regarding the listing of church property for tax purposes, particularly in states requiring an annual application and when church property has been bought or sold or its use changed.

LEGAL TITLE TO CHURCH PROPERTY

In most states, an unincorporated church is legally considered to be an association that can receive and hold title and dispose of property only through trustees or other representatives acting on behalf of the association. Incorporation, where feasible, secures the advantages of continuity and the exemption of church members from personal financial liability for acts of the corporation. The incorporated church is a legal entity with powers distinct from its component members. Churches that are not legally incorporated, but by state law can be, probably should proceed with incorporation.

The property management committee of a church considering the purchase of real estate should assure itself that the title to the property in question is clear of encumbrances.[1] Any restrictions in the deeds and any easements, reversionary clauses, or other limitations should be carefully considered.

The church should not accept or purchase property

[1] See page 41 for suggested duties of the property management committee.

without approval of its property management committee. The committee should evaluate the condition, location, appropriateness, restrictions on use, and the anticipated continuing costs involved in receiving or purchasing additional property—whether land, buildings, furnishings, or equipment.

PLANNING FULL USE OF CHURCH BUILDINGS

Many church buildings remain unused much of the week. An idle church building should challenge congregational leadership to reexamine the church's concept of its purpose in the light of the spiritual needs of the community. Such careful study could lead to a more effective and comprehensive ministry both to its own members and to other people.

Multiple use should be made of available space whenever possible. This may involve conducting two or three successive worship services and church school sessions a week. Such multiple use of limited space usually makes increased demands on the budget for costs involved in the rearrangement of equipment, for additional cleaning, and for utilities needed. These expenses are negligible, however, when compared with the cost of constructing and maintaining separate facilities for each church-related and community activity.

Before a church plunges into a building project, careful study should be given to setting forth a master plan that relates to the goals and program of the church. Present facilities should be evaluated, using a space-utilization work sheet, to discover satisfactory ways of fitting the proposed program into existing facilities before deciding to build or remodel.

BASIC USES OF CHURCH PROPERTY

We believe that the basic use of church property should be for worship, education, and fellowship. Each congregation should determine its goals and structure its program of use and maintenance of property best to realize these objectives. Each congregation should determine its own scale of priorities. A small congregation with limited resources may decide to build a church with a multipurpose meeting room suitable for worship and adaptable for programs of education and fellowship. In keeping with the principle of multiple use, dining areas may be used for education purposes at one time, and recreation purposes at another.

PROVIDE FOR SPECIAL GROUPS

Weekday activities for all ages, providing an appropriate hour of Bible study, assistance with personal and family problems, Christian fellowship, recreational activities, and other needed ministries make good use of church facilities and bring the church into a meaningful relation to human need. Small "cell groups" may use the church buildings for prayer, Bible study, meditation, and Christian fellowship.

Many churches now provide a program of graded choirs by age groupings with scheduled rehearsals at various times during the week. Such choral groups train large numbers of people in meaningful worship through music. Midweek worship services are frequently provided. These services may be preceded by meetings of the church school officers and teachers or other leadership groups desiring to make intensive preparation for teaching periods on the following Sunday. Meetings should be purposeful and should contribute to the achievement of church objectives. Whatever meetings are needed to accomplish these objectives should be provided to the extent that the resources of the church will permit.

RECREATION ACTIVITIES

Good management of church recreation facilities requires clearly formulated rules and regulations and adequate provision for supervision and control. The property management committee should be consulted to insure provision of appropriate measures for proper care of church property.

Churches that may not have sufficient financial resources to construct recreation buildings can often make multiple use of existing space and thus provide facilities for many forms of recreation. New equipment, materials, and techniques aid in converting present space to such use. Tough vinyl-plastic fabrics can be applied to wall surfaces. Colorful and durable floor tile can add beauty. Special tile kits are available for installing shuffleboard courts in the floor tile pattern. Acoustical treatment of walls and ceilings can help overcome noise problems.

TYPES OF RECREATION ACTIVITIES

Four basic types of activities are usually included or desired in a church recreation program—socials, creative arts and crafts, drama, and athletics. Social activities such as class parties with group games require very little adaptation of facilities. A room with movable chairs and a piano is usually adequate. Facilities for serving refreshments are desirable. Cultural recreation, such as discussion groups, can conveniently be accommodated in church education facilities or parlors. A church library provides for leisure-time reading. Church camping may call for some church-owned camping equipment if campers are not prepared to supply their own.

Creative arts and crafts require some special equipment. If interest and funds are sufficient, more elaborate facilities may be provided, with electrical tools, ceramic kilns, sinks, worktables, and storage areas.

Drama need not be confined to church dramatic clubs involving only a few highly motivated individuals. It can be used as an effective learning device by church groups of all ages. All departments should be encouraged to use drama, adapting as necessary to provide the needed settings. As resources are available, drama facilities may be provided in a multipurpose room. The stage should be from two to three feet high, enabling actors to be seen from all areas of the room. Overhead lighting placed well in front of the stage to provide 45-degree spotlighting is desirable. Flexible arrangements are preferable to large fixed spotlights. Lights should be controlled from a switch panel and rheostat offstage.

The church can conduct many athletic activities without having to build a gymnasium. Although it is desirable to have a gymnasium, if other facilities deserve a higher priority, church leaders should recognize the high cost of maintaining a gymnasium and providing the personal supervision essential to effective use.

Whether a church has a recreation building of its own need not determine the scope of the athletic program. In many cases a gymnasium can be obtained for church use from schools or other community agencies. Many outdoor athletic programs do not require a gymnasium. Good leadership, creative planning, and interested participants can overcome many limitations.

DESIGN FOR RECREATION SPACE

For maximum use with greatest economy, recreation areas in churches should be built as multipurpose rooms. The same area may be effectively used as a fellowship hall, drama theater, roller-skating area, gymnasium, and education assembly area.

Church recreation activities require supervision. A centralized supervisor's station with visibility into recreation areas will reduce the size of the staff required. Remote activity or craft rooms, unsupervised corridors, or scattered recreation areas create supervisory problems. The preferred location for the supervisor's station in the church recreation area is near the outside entrance and adjacent to the play areas. Glass panels should permit observation of activities in progress. By locating the supervisor's station near the entrance, access to and from the recreation area can be better controlled. Preferably, other areas of the building are closed off so that those coming for recreation activities are not free to go into other sections of the building.

Areas to be used for recreation should be suitably constructed or remodeled. In gymnasium areas all light fixtures and windows should be protected with specially designed wire screens. Soft acoustical plaster is easily damaged by balls or other flying objects. Porous unglazed tiles or flat paints on walls and ceilings are too easily soiled.

Recreation areas require adequate storage for sports equipment, tables, uniforms, craft-shop equipment, camping equipment, drama equipment, and stage sets. Where multiple use is made of any area it is particularly important to have readily available storage areas to facilitate the quick shifts that are sometimes required.

Floor materials for recreation areas should be of a type best suited to the several activities to be conducted in the area. By using an appropriate finish on a hardwood gymnasium floor, it is possible to use it for roller-skating, as a gymnasium, and even as a dining hall.

If recreation areas are not to be used for basketball or volleyball, the ceiling height of rooms need not be extremely high. For dramatics, a rectangular room with a stage or platform across one of the narrow ends is preferred, with a ratio of five feet in length to three feet in width. A minimum of ten feet in ceiling height is needed for rooms up to fifty feet long—twelve feet or more for those of greater length. Recessed lighting in ceiling panels gives an impression of greater height and does not obstruct recreation activities.

RENTAL POLICIES

Many churches with gymnasium facilities have policies and rental schedules for outside groups. Fees are usually charged to underwrite the costs of supervision, janitor service, and physical maintenance.

In one church, outside groups are charged a fee of five dollars per hour for basketball practice or game time. Fees for other activities are set according to the area used, the duration of the activity, and the supervision and janitor service required. For roller-skating parties, the charge is twenty-five cents per person per hour or five dollars per hour total minimum charge. Each group using the gymnasium in this church is required to provide adequate leadership responsible for the proper use of the facilities. Any outside groups are required to make their reservations through a designated member of the church owning the gymnasium. This church member serves as a sponsor for the group and is required to be in attendance when the gymnasium is being used by the group making a reservation through him.

The use of a badge-card attendance-checking system identifies those who have permission to use recreation facilities, serves as a method of screening those who need the attention of supervisors, and provides a means of checking the use of facilities. A card is issued to those qualified to use the recreation facilities. As each one enters, he checks his number on a check-in sheet and obtains his badge, which is worn during the time the individual is in the recreation area. Cards are left as deposits when game equipment is checked out and are returned to the individual when he brings back the equipment in good condition.

Church Weddings: Members of the congregation should be encouraged to use the church for weddings. Marriage is one of the most significant events of life, and it should be conducted with the blessing of the church. Young people contemplating marriage should know that their church wishes to join them in this high and holy hour. The building and staff of the church should be available for the happy occasion of marriage. Even private weddings may appropriately be held in the church sanctuary or chapel.

Some churches prefer to make their facilities available without charge to members of their own congregation. Some suggest remuneration for staff members performing additional work. Specific information as to what is expected and what is provided should be given to couples planning a wedding.

Weddings of Nonchurch Members: Each church should determine and have on record its policy concerning the use of the church buildings for the marriage of nonmembers. Many churches have found it useful to prepare a printed folder giving full information regarding church policy and setting forth in detail regulations regarding the use of the buildings, including information regarding floral decorations, candles, wedding receptions, and any fee to be provided for the participating ministers, musicians, janitorial staff, or other costs.

A booklet giving full information on weddings in the church can be quite useful for those planning church weddings, whether members of the congregation or not. Sometimes people are careless or uninformed about appropriate procedures in the use of church facilities. Consequently, many churches have adopted specific regulations regarding decorations, moving of furniture, the taking of photographs, the use of rice or confetti, and appropriate behavior of members of the wedding party.

The church staff or property management committee should prepare such information for inclusion in a church operations manual. Separate sections should be available to give to couples planning a wedding, to the florist, to the photographer, and to the caterer in charge of the reception. The following items should be explained in a booklet or instruction sheet:

1. How to reserve the chapel or the sanctuary
2. Procedure for scheduling services of minister and music personnel
3. Requirements regarding premarital counseling sessions
4. Fees charged to members and nonmembers for formal and informal weddings
5. Regulations regarding permissible decorations
6. Schedule and conduct of rehearsals
7. Regulations regarding smoking and use of alcoholic beverages
8. Photographing the wedding and reception

Instructions to the florist should be specific. A deposit to cover possible damage may be required. Instructions may include information regarding the number and placement of floral arrangements, candelabra, kneeling bench, candles, aisle carpets, dressing-room use, and cleaning of church property after the wedding.

Regulations regarding wedding receptions should indicate the facilities that can be furnished by the church and the cost of various services and equipment. Time limits, both before and after the reception, should be stated.

Funerals in the Church: Death in a family is a crisis that the church should seek to meet with sympathetic understanding and helpfulness. One evidence of concern is that of making available the use of the church buildings for funeral services. Experienced funeral directors are generally careful to observe acceptable practices in the use of the church buildings, making the establishing of extensive regulations unnecessary. It is appropriate, however, for the church to approve and distribute to families and funeral directors information about any regulations, fees, or other requirements involved in the use of the church buildings for funerals.

Religious Services for Other Groups: Sometimes churches are asked to permit the use of their buildings for religious services of other churches or religious groups. Invitations to denominational or interdenominational groups, or requests from sister churches with inadequate facilities, for the use of the church buildings suggest the wisdom of having a church-adopted policy, clearly stated, as to how such invitations will be extended or requests approved.

Community Meetings in Church Buildings: To what extent should the church buildings be made available to community organizations for their meetings? Churches with well-equipped social rooms, dining facilities, recreation facilities, or commodious auditoriums usually have frequent requests for the use of their facilities. Such meetings often involve the use of expensive equipment by untrained amateurs. Churches usually need carefully drawn regulations regarding the use of their facilities by other groups, if such use is to be permitted. Use of the building should normally be restricted to those activities consistent with the program, ideals, and philosophy of the church.

ESTABLISH REGULATIONS

Who is to determine the policy of the church in regard to the use of the church facilities? Such a policy should be set by a responsible group that has carefully considered all aspects of the matter. Since operational procedures of churches differ widely, no effort is made here to specify which group should determine or execute the policies on church use. Whether such policies are determined by the congregation, the official board, a church committee, or a specific church official, they should be written and on file for ready reference whenever the occasion arises.

In some churches the pastor or some other staff member may be authorized to handle all requests for use of church facilities. Others may use a committee to deal with such requests, committee decisions being subject to review or approval by the congregation or the official board. Because of the changes that may occur in staff personnel, regulations should be recorded as a guide for those making these decisions.

In preparing regulations for use of church facilities some system of priorities may appropriately be used. If there are conflicting requests, preference may be given to activities of the church congregation rather than non-congregational meetings. Priority may be given to activities in certain areas involving larger groups or the total congregation, instead of smaller groups that might be able to use other rooms. A regularly scheduled meeting should normally hold precedence over a special or occasional meeting unless the customary group has decided not to meet at the usual time and place.

MAINTAIN A MASTER CALENDAR

A member of the church staff, usually a secretary, should be designated as the keeper of the official calendar for scheduling use of church facilities. Policies regarding the use of the building should be made clear to all requesting use of space. The First Baptist Church of Shreveport, Louisiana,[1] makes the following types of forms available for such requests:

REQUESTS FOR FACILITIES AND DATE ON CHURCH CALENDAR

(This form must be completed and returned to the church office before any meeting in the church building can be scheduled and listed on the church calendar.)

[1] Used by permission.

Attention: Building Superintendent

Organization_____Type of Meeting_____

Person in Charge_____Phone_____

    Date of Meeting_____Rooms Required_____

    Hours of Meeting___to___Number Expected to Attend___

Facilities Needed and Special Instructions_____

    (Please detail special requirements and equipment to be used.)

_____

_____

Checked by_____Approved_____Date_____

FIRST BAPTIST CHURCH—SHREVEPORT

REQUEST FOR FOOD SERVICE

    (At least 2 days notice is required for any type food service.)

Attention: Church Hostess

Organization_____Type of Meal_____

Person in Charge_____Phone_____

    Date of Meal_____ Suggested Menu and Special

                        Instructions

    Time of Meal_____ _____

    Place_____ _____

    Number Reservations___ _____

    (Please confirm 24 hours

    in advance)

    Price per Plate_____ _____

    (To be approved by

    Hostess) _____

This date cleared on Calendar____Approved___Date___

FIRST BAPTIST CHURCH—SHREVEPORT

REQUEST FOR NURSERY

Attention: Nursery Coordinator
Organization_____Person in Charge_____Date_____
   Date of Activity_____Number of Children_____
   Time of Activity__to__Ages of Children:
   Place of Meeting_____Babies_____Toddlers_____
                        2 yr. olds_____3 yr. olds_____

Checked and Approved_____Date_____
FIRST BAPTIST CHURCH—SHREVEPORT

The church may wish to stipulate just what is permissible in various areas of the building. For example, if smoking is forbidden, this should be indicated in the regulations.

If fees are charged for the use of the building and for payment of custodial personnel, information as to the amount and time of required payment should be supplied to those requesting use of church facilities before permission is given. A responsible official of any nonchurch group desiring to use church facilities should sign a request form indicating the date, hour, approximate number expected, and facilities needed. This form should include a pledge to abide by church regulations on use of the building, to give proper care to church facilities, and to leave them clean and properly arranged after use.

Property used either by the church or by other groups having church permission to engage in profit-making sales or similar enterprises may involve tax liability not otherwise incurred. Church officials should carefully study laws in each state and community regarding such matters.

Schedule Rooms by Number: Each room in the church building should be numbered. The church office and the custodian's office should each have a list of the rooms. This list should show the number of the room on the left

Figure 1

Room Assignment Record

c=chair,
t=table, oo"=height

Room No. or name	Sunday	Monday	Tuesday	Wednesday	Thursday	Friday	Saturday	Equipment
1	9–11 A.M. Primary II SS 6–7:30 P.M. Primary I			6:30 P.M. Missionary Education			10 A.M. Primary Choir	20c 14" 2t Piano 24"
2								
3								
4								
5								
6	Junior I 9–11 A.M. 5–6 P.M. Junior Choir 6–6:30 P.M. Junior T.U.	3 P.M. Weekday Bible Class		6:30 P.M. Junior Missionary Education				
101	Adult I	City Pastor's Conference		6:30 P.M. Teachers Meeting				
102								
201	9–11 A.M. Young People 9–10:30 P.M. Youth Fellowship			6:30 P.M. Teachers Meeting		10 P.M. after–game fellowship		
202								

side of the sheet. In columns to the right should be entered the regularly scheduled uses made of each room and its furniture and other equipment. The Room Assignment Record form in Figure 1 is partially completed to illustrate its use.

Before scheduling any room for use by any group, the responsible person should determine its availability and suitability for the meeting requested.

USE OF MUSICAL INSTRUMENTS

Should members of the church congregation be permitted to practice on church organs or pianos? Some churches permit the organist to give organ instruction to private pupils, allowing use of the church instrument for both lessons and practice. Others do not permit any use except by the church organist when preparing for church services. Policies regarding such matters should be set after consultation with the music committee and the organist.

SECURITY AND PROTECTION MEASURES [2]

Unfortunately, serious problems of vandalism, theft, and other forms of damage to property and threats to persons necessitate protective measures in some communities. Security measures involve maintenance employees, for they are usually responsible for locking and unlocking the building on a predetermined schedule. It may be necessary to keep locked all areas of the building not in use. Some churches have employed night watchmen to supplement the maintenance staff in keeping an around-the-clock watch over church properties.

Churches experiencing difficulties in the protection of property or persons should consult police authorities regarding protective and preventive measures that might

[2] For a contrary view see William Folprecht, "Let's Unlock Our Church Doors," *Church Management*, XXXVII, No. 7 (1961) pp. 30-31.

be taken. One church that had experienced difficulty not
only with vandalism but also from thoughtless abuse of
church facilities by those attending various church activities printed the following statement in the weekly
church paper distributed to its entire membership:

TO INSURE THE BEST USE OF
SPACE AND EQUIPMENT [3]

At its meeting November 21, the House Committee authorized the installation of locks on most inside doors
which do not now have them. Thereafter it will be the
policy of the Committee to maintain the security of all
rooms except as their use may be authorized by the
Church Use Committee of the Board of Deacons. This is
an extension of the policy now being pursued on those
rooms which already have locks.

Locking our doors is deplored in principle, but as a matter of practical necessity it is believed to be the most effective, most economical, and most objective method of
protecting the property and privileges of our members.
The obvious problem this would help to control is mali-
cious vandalism by those who lack respect for the Church
and its message. While severe when it occurs, such vandalism is a rather uncommon, infrequent complaint.

More often our difficulties have occurred when well-
intentioned but perhaps thoughtless people have used a
room without notice, removed or disarranged furnishings
or equipment, damaged class work projects, or otherwise
created some irritant disturbing to the teacher or leader of
the groups for whom the space is primarily provided.

This action represents no retreat from our established
policy of "multiple use." Upon making proper reservations
through the Church Office, any officially recognized
church organization will be granted permission to use any

[3] Reprinted by permission from bulletin of First Baptist Church, Washington, D.C.

appropriate space for its activities at any time when there will not be interference with others. Any teacher or other church worker will have access to his work area for preparation, study, arrangements, etc.

It is the Committee's purpose to assure that rooms will be occupied only with the advance knowledge of the Building Superintendent so that adequate preparation can be made for cleaning and restoring the space for subsequent use. As a general rule, the Business Manager has been asked to avoid assigning space on Saturday night if the actvity will require substantial custodial work to condition it for Sunday.

Wherever circumstances indicate that some of the church entrance doors should be kept locked, a small notice may be securely fastened on or near such doors indicating the location of another entrance and the hours when it is open, for example:

Welcome to Christ Church.
If this door is locked please go to entrance on
Main Street, open 8:00 A.M. to 5:00 P.M.

LENDING CHURCH EQUIPMENT

Lending church equipment, as a general practice, should be discouraged. If equipment is loaned, however, a careful record should be maintained, indicating the item on loan, the place to which it is to be taken, and the organization by which it is to be used. The record should bear the signature of a responsible individual guaranteeing safe and prompt return of the equipment.

As suggested earlier, each item of church equipment should be labeled and numbered, and an inventory record should specify where that item is to be kept. When a piece of equipment is loaned, its inventory number should be recorded on the checkout sheet—to be checked off the list when the item is returned.

When the church rents or leases property for church use, it should be careful to maintain the property in good condition. Written agreements clearly stating responsibility for redecoration, custodial care, and use and repair of equipment should be drawn up and approved by proper church authorities and the owner of the property.

Chapter Summary

1. Church buildings should be fully utilized for maximum results in achieving church objectives.

2. Ways of using or adapting present facilities, instead of constructing new buildings, should be evaluated carefully in seeking space for new or expanded programs.

3. A carefully coordinated calendar and a space utilization chart can enable the church to provide space for numerous programs and activities of its own, and, when consistent with church objectives, for community groups as well.

4. All rooms in the church building should be numbered, and a room assignment chart should show the use of each room at various times during the week.

Chapter 2

MAINTAINING
CHURCH PROPERTY

AN ADEQUATE maintenance program keeps buildings, equipment, and grounds at or near their original condition of completeness or efficiency. It provides for routine operation of the buildings, keeping them properly cleaned, heated or cooled and arranged for needed use. It includes care of the grounds and parking areas, and the protection of all church-owned buildings and equipment.

SEVEN TARGETS IN MAINTENANCE

1. *Cleanliness and utility:* Church property should be kept in condition to serve effectively the varied needs of the church. Church buildings should provide an environment conducive to worship, education, fellowship, and service. They must be kept properly lighted, heated or cooled, cleaned, and free of avoidable hazards to the health and welfare of all who use them.

2. *Multiple use of facilities:* Church buildings can serve many different church groups if needed changes are made in the arrangement of furnishings and equipment. A meeting room for education groups can be converted into a dining room by bringing in tables and shifting the chairs. By removing the tables and chairs, the room can be converted into a recreation area. Such multiple use of rooms

is greatly facilitated if storage space for tables, chairs, recreation equipment, and other supplies is conveniently located.

3. *Economy in operation of facilities:* Good maintenance corrects conditions causing waste and excessive costs of heating, cooling, or other utilities. Plumbing, heating, air conditioning, and electrical systems must be kept in proper operating condition for greatest efficiency and economy. Selecting the correct size and type of light bulbs, turning off unnecessary lights, and controlling heating and cooling can affect operation expenses favorably. Dirty windows and light fixtures reduce light intensity considerably. Periodic washing of windows and fixtures can be less expensive than using higher-wattage bulbs. Thousands of gallons of water can be wasted because of faulty plumbing. If this water has been heated, a waste of fuel is also involved.

Proper purchase, storage, and distribution of maintenance supplies improves operating efficiency and reduces expenses. Proper maintenance prolongs equipment life and ensures better performance. Orderly storage in protected and secure locations reduces risk of vandalism and theft.

4. *Safeguards against injury and accident:* Many injury-producing accidents are the result of defective equipment, deterioration or poor construction. Improperly treated floors or a defective stair or sidewalk may cause a serious fall. Good maintenance will locate and eliminate such hazards.

5. *Health and welfare benefits:* The health and safety of those using church property can be enhanced by proper sanitary conditions and by healthy levels of temperature, humidity, ventilation, and lighting.

6. *Protection of investment:* The proverb "A stitch in time saves nine" is particularly applicable to the repair of leaking roofs, sagging gutters, faulty plumbing, or defective wiring. Timely maintenance prevents premature

deterioration of buildings. It protects buildings from losses by fire, abuse, and vandalism. A less expensive insurance rating is often available when high standards of maintenance prevail.

7. *Building a good image:* A dusty pew, a broken chair, peeling paint, dirty windows, or shabby landscaping discourage the appreciation and respect that lead to one's identification with a church. Poorly maintained buildings make it difficult for the church to accomplish its basic objectives. Clean, comfortable buildings encourage meaningful worship, effective learning, and high morale. Favorable community reaction is facilitated by efficient property management.

WHO'S IN CHARGE?

To whom shall the church entrust the care and upkeep of its property? What organization structure within the church is needed to establish and supervise an adequate program of church property maintenance? The suggestions that follow provide guidelines that may be helpful in answering these questions.

Each church should have a property management committee for over-all supervision of the maintenance program. Churches employing a business manager should delegate this responsibility to him. A church would not be investing its ministerial resources wisely if its pastor were involved many hours each week in giving close supervision to maintenance personnel. Adequate supervision of maintenance must be provided by the property management committee, the business manager, or some other member of the church staff.

CHAIN OF COMMAND

Church employees may feel they have as many "bosses" as there are church members. Yet, there ought never really to be any doubt as to the person or persons to whom each one is responsible. This line of authority and supervisory control should be clear both to the employees and the church official in a supervisory capacity.

The good nature and helpful attitude of some maintenance workers may involve them in so many errands and extra duties for others that they are unable to accomplish their regular maintenance duties satisfactorily. Yet for them to refuse repeated requests for work not officially assigned them may create ill will and misunderstanding. It is therefore essential that a job description be carefully prepared for each maintenance employee, and that requests for other work be referred to the maintenance supervisor or to the church committee directing the maintenance program. It may be necessary in some cases to include in the job description specific tasks that the worker should not perform without definite instructions from his supervisor. Such a procedure would help to free the employee from pressures to perform extraneous duties that would hinder the proper performance of his assigned tasks.

Some of the members of the property management committee should be familiar with standard practices in the cleaning and operation of the buildings. The congregation or its appropriate governing bodies can aid immeasurably in providing an adequate maintenance program by selecting a suitable committee or a well-informed staff member to supervise the work and the workers.

PROPERTY MANAGEMENT COMMITTEE DUTIES

1. Determine by careful inspection the condition of the church property.

2. Locate mechanical and structural faults, if possible before they become serious, and institute remedial procedures.

3. Communicate to the budget committee a careful estimate of funds needed for current operation, and for anticipated major replacements.

4. Determine and recommend to the church governing body the kind and number of employees needed to maintain church properties in attractive, sanitary, and usable condition.

5. Establish work standards and schedules for maintenance personnel.

6. Determine priorities and set up a schedule for property repairs, replacements, and additions.

7. Inspect buildings for fire hazards, and secure and maintain adequate fire control equipment.

8. Recommend purchases of equipment and supplies for preventive maintenance.

9. Inspect and inventory all church property, maintaining up-to-date records on all additions and dispositions of such property.

PROPERTY MANAGEMENT COMMITTEE AT WORK

The property management committee is responsible for developing policies, for inspecting maintenance work, and, in some cases, for giving direct supervision to the maintenance staff. Its work relates to all aspects of care and upkeep of buildings, equipment, and grounds. It reports to the church governing body regarding the condition of the building, needed changes in personnel, replacements for equipment or buildings, repairs and redecoration needed, and problems related to the use of the buildings, equipment, or other facilities. The supervisor designated by the church to give direct oversight to the work of the maintenance staff may sometimes be the chairman of the property management committee. The chairman of the property management committee serves also as the channel through which complaints or commendations are received from the church membership concerning matters pertaining to maintenance of property.

In organizing itself and its work, the property management committee should determine what assignments it has received from the church. If there is no written description of the committee's work, it might wisely formulate its own job description and present it to the church government body with the query, "Is this what you would like the property management committee to do?" After discussion, consultation, and changes (if necessary), this could be adopted.

Important functions of the property management committee include evaluating the performance of employees and establishing work standards. Low productivity may be due to poor training, inexperience, poor equipment, inadequate and inconveniently located storage rooms for supplies and equipment, or deteriorated property. It may be necessary in some cases to replace incompetent or disabled workers. If so, the property management committee should be involved in attracting, interviewing, employing, and training new workers. Although the committee may not personally interview, hire, or dismiss workers, it should certainly recommend policies for obtaining and retaining maintenance personnel.

The committee may need to correct any purchasing practices that handicap the procurement of needed tools and supplies. When improved practices and equipment are introduced, the committee should insist that they be used as directed. Everyone tends to resist change and to revert to familiar ways of doing things, but such problems should not be permitted to jeopardize the whole program of improved maintenance.

SECURE COOPERATION OF
ORGANIZATION LEADERS

If church property were never used, there would not be much need for cleaning. The people who use the property create the soil load that makes cleaning necessary. If those who use church property are aware of the effect of increased soil load on the quality and cost of cleaning, they can help reduce considerably the soil load that must be removed.

Members of the congregation should be made aware of ways they can help keep their church clean, orderly, and attractive. Teachers and program leaders can be encouraged to remove papers, books, and other materials from tabletops and desks, so that furniture can be cleaned quickly and thoroughly. Groups working on projects of various kinds can be encouraged to spend the closing minutes of each period in cleaning up the area. More adequate storage space should be provided if needed.

Church members should also be encouraged to express appreciation to the maintenance staff for work well done. Such appreciation, coupled with efforts to cooperate in keeping the property clean, will gladden the hearts of employees, who too often hear only complaints.

USING VOLUNTEER HELPERS

What about the small church that does not have, and feels it cannot afford, a paid janitor even on a part-time basis? Many such churches resolve the problem by using volunteer help of their members and friends. Twelve families may agree to take one month each as their responsibility for upkeep and care of the church property. Periodic maintenance—such as painting and the washing of walls, ceilings, woodwork, and windows—may be done by special groups on work days. Such occasions can provide enjoyable social fellowship.

Whether using paid help or volunteer labor, each church needs a property management committee to plan the work, to obtain the needed supplies, and to assume continuing responsibility for keeping the property in attractive, usable condition.

HOW LARGE A MAINTENANCE STAFF?

One of the responsibilities of the property management committee is to determine the size of the maintenance staff. Factors affecting this decision may include: location, size, and condition of the property; frequency of property use and the equipment provided; and the ability, skill, and motivation of available workers.

A church whose buildings are set in the midst of several beautifully landscaped acres may require many man-hours of labor weekly to care for lawns, shrubs, flowers, walks, driveways, and parking areas. Formal gardens and other attractive features require constant attention at certain seasons of the year. Removal of snow from walks, driveways, and parking areas makes other demands upon the custodian's time. Play equipment, inside or outside, subjected to hard use, requires repairs, adjustments, and inspection for safety and cleanliness.

For large buildings frequently used by various groups that require shifts of equipment, a large maintenance staff is needed. To reduce the number of maintenance workers needed, weekday activities that do not utilize the entire building can be concentrated in a single building or floor, rather than scattered over several areas.

The age and condition of the building, furnishings, fixtures, and equipment make considerable difference in maintenance time required. Minor repairs must be made more frequently as a building grows older. Major breakdowns throw routine maintenance operations off schedule. Floors, walls, and furniture that have become scratched or marred through years of use are more difficult to keep clean and attractive.

The kinds and amount of maintenance required vary according to the equipment to be taken care of and the way it was installed. Central air-conditioning equipment may require the maintenance services of a competent engineer. Converting heating equipment from use of coal to use of gas or oil usually reduces considerably the man-hours required for operation.

The type of equipment and furnishings influences the cost of cleaning. Movable chairs and tables make floor cleaning much easier. Wall-mounted blackboards, cork boards, tack boards, and picture rails or clips are more convenient than easels or other floor-mounted items from the standpoint of moving and cleaning.

The use of labor-saving equipment, such as floor sweepers, scrubbers, buffers, or power mowers, may reduce the size of staff needed to maintain the building and grounds satisfactorily.

BLUEPRINT OF MAINTENANCE PERSONNEL RELATIONSHIPS

The property management committee should survey the amount of maintenance work to be done and estimate the number of people required to do it. The church governing body should designate the person to supervise the maintenance work. One good way of clarifying these relationships is to prepare an organization chart showing the place of the maintenance staff in the total picture. Such a chart is helpful to employees, who need to know to whom they are responsible for instructions and supervision. Employees should know how to report emergencies, request supplies, and obtain information about coming events that require use of physical facilities.

A good organization chart will help each employee recognize that he is part of a team contributing to the total success of the church. When an employee understands his particular responsibility and its relationship to other aspects of the church program, he can cooperate more intelligently with other staff members and can see why he is asked to perform certain tasks. Each church should design its own organization chart to reflect both its own pattern

Figure 2

Example of Organization Chart for Church with Small Custodial Staff*

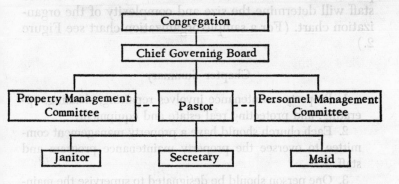

Example of Organization Chart for Church with Large Custodial Staff*

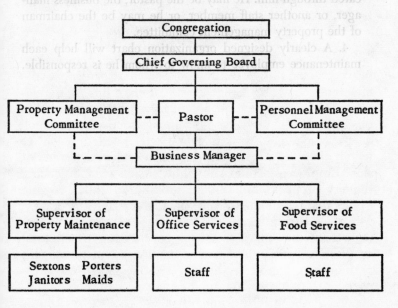

*Courtesy of the Center for Church Business Management, The American University, Washington, D. C.

of church government and the responsibilities of church personnel. The size of the church and of its maintenance staff will determine the size and complexity of the organization chart. (For a sample organization chart see Figure 2.)

Chapter Summary

1. Property maintenance involves repairing, cleaning, operating, and protecting real estate and equipment.

2. Each church should have a property management committee to oversee the property maintenance program and staff.

3. One person should be designated to supervise the maintenance program. All instructions should be communicated through him. He may be the pastor, the business manager, or another staff member, or he may be the chairman of the property management committee.

4. A clearly designed organization chart will help each maintenance employee to know to whom he is responsible.

Chapter 3

EMPLOYING
MAINTENANCE PERSONNEL

EMPLOYMENT POLICIES AND PROCEDURES

THE FIRST STEP in employing a maintenance worker is to prepare or revise a job description. If there are two or more employees, it may be wise to rearrange responsibilities. Prospective employees want to know exactly what is expected of them, and what is offered in salary and fringe benefits.

Policies regarding employment of staff personnel should be established by the governing body of the church. They should indicate any limitations regarding who may be employed. For instance, what is or should be the policy of the church regarding the religious affiliation of members of the maintenance staff? Age, race, sex, education, experience, personal habits, recommendations from previous employers, and performance on simple tests are examples of items that may be involved in personnel policies. These policies should not be so rigid and idealistic as to make it impossible to obtain employees, but the standards should be high enough that obviously incompetent people will not be employed.

When it is certain that a new employee is needed, and when his duties are clearly defined, the church is then ready to consider candidates for the job. The church office

49

should keep for the personnel committee or the property management committee, or both, a list of persons who may have expressed an interest in employment for maintenance work. School administrators can often give information about available maintenance personnel. Employment offices can usually supply recommendations. Retired military personnel are often available for such work and are usually competent workers.

USE AN APPLICATION FORM

An application form should be filled out by each person being considered for employment. This form should indicate age, sex, marital status, height, weight, former employers, education, training and experience in maintenance, length of service on each previous job, when available to begin work, condition of health, physical handicaps, and other relevant information.

The application form may be accompanied by a brief objective test covering basic information one would need to function effectively in the particular position. Such a test should indicate the applicant's ability to write and to follow directions and his knowledge of maintenance materials, equipment, and skills.

INTERVIEW THE APPLICANT

All applicants should be interviewed by one or more members of the personnel committee and by the supervisor under whose direction he would work. No one should be employed without the approval of the church-designated supervisor. The interview should reveal the personality traits of the applicant, his alertness, his interest in the work, and his abilities in property maintenance.

Maintenance employees should possess *capacity to learn.* This does not mean that they must have extensive academic training, although such might be helpful. They should be able to understand the reasons for doing certain tasks, the appropriate time and circumstances for doing them, and the implications of the work required.

Maintenance personnel should be in *good health* and physically able to do the heavy work involved. Poor eyesight, deafness, heart trouble, and other physical handicaps make it difficult, if not impossible, to function satisfactorily. Overweight persons often have difficulty in bending and in climbing stairs and ladders, and they usually move slowly.

Maintenance personnel should be of *good character*. Personal habits, purity of life and language, courtesy, cleanliness, cooperativeness, tact, loyalty, and dependability are essential to good work and good relationships.

The ability to *get along with people,* not only with the supervisor and other church employees, but also with all who use the church facilities, is very important. Although it is not necessary, and sometimes not wise, to employ members of the congregation as workers in their own church, employees who are committed to the ideals and goals the church is seeking to achieve will probably work more diligently and conscientiously. Morale and a spirit of teamwork is much more likely to prevail when employees view their work as a means of service to their fellow man and to God, as well as a way of earning a living.

EVALUATE APPLICANT'S QUALIFICATIONS

Church leaders should study the applications and the test results of all prospective employees. On the basis of this information and impressions gained from personal interviews, and from evaluations expressed by former employers, preferably in private conversations, decisions should be made regarding the best-qualified applicant.

If there is doubt about the applicant's qualifications, it may be wise to set up the first few months as a probationary period. If his work and his relations with others are satisfactory throughout the probationary period, he may then be placed on continuing status with full staff benefits.

It is much easier, less embarrassing—and a better stewardship of responsibility—to choose employees carefully and to screen out unsatisfactory persons before employment rather than to dismiss them after they have proved unsuitable for the job. Potentially capable people, under proper conditions and motivations, can grow on the job. Usually they will respond to training and, with experience, become dependable, skilled employees. Incompetent people require more supervision, make costly mistakes, and often cause dissatisfaction among the church members. Because of sympathy for such people or for their families they might be kept on the church payroll long after their basic inabilities have become apparent. Half the problems of property maintenance are solved when capable employees are enlisted and properly trained for their tasks.

PROVIDE EMPLOYMENT REGULATIONS

A written statement of regulations such as the following should be provided for each employee:

Hours of Work
(Schedule determined by particular job and local circumstances.)

Payday
Salary checks are issued on the fifteenth day and the last day of each month.

Withholdings from Wages
Minimum legal amounts are withheld for social security benefits, for federal and state income taxes, and for employee's portion of insurance and pension plans.

Rest Periods
A 15-minute rest period or coffee break is provided each morning and each afternoon for the comfort and refreshment of employee.

Solicitations for Gifts or Sales

Solicitation of funds among employees shall be limited to such events as retirement, termination, or marriage of a fellow employee. Salesmen should see employees outside working hours regarding personal matters.

Illness or Injury

If an employee becomes ill on the job or is injured in any way, his supervisor should be informed immediately so that arrangements may be made for the employee to go home or to visit a physician.

Absence from Work

When kept from work by illness or other unavoidable reason, the employee should inform his supervisor immediately, giving reasons for the absence and stating when he expects to return to work. In the case of death of a member of the immediate family, the employee is paid during his absence, for a period not to exceed one week. In case of the death of relatives other than the immediate family, the employee is paid for absence on the day of the funeral.

NAME THE JOB

Many different titles are used for church maintenance employees. Most frequently used are the terms *janitor, custodian,* and *sexton.* All have interesting histories. *Janitor* is related to the Latin word for *door* and to the Roman deity, Janus, who presided over doors and gates. Janus was usually depicted as having two faces looking in opposite directions. The word *sexton* derives from *sacristan,* which refers to an official or employee of a church who is responsible for taking care of the church edifice and its contents. The word *custodian* is derived from the Greek word *custos,* meaning guardian of properties and values. His job is that of protecting the physical plant and the people using it, by means of adequate safeguards, proper sanitation, and cleanliness.

In some churches one may also hear such titles as plant engineer, maintenance supervisor, superintendent of buildings and grounds, and property manager. The work of the maintenance staff may be divided into two or more special classifications to care for cleaning, operation, repairs, and food service. Whatever the job title, it should indicate the kinds of duties and responsibilities required.

DESCRIBE THE JOB

Accurate job titles, adequate job descriptions, good organization charts, and detailed work schedules should enable each maintenance employee to know what he is supposed to do and to whom he is responsible. Problems with maintenance employees usually are attributable to misunderstandings about the exact duties expected, and by whom and at what time the work is to be done. Much confusion can be avoided by the preparation and use of job descriptions and work schedules that state clearly the duties to be performed, how the work is to be done, the tools and machines to be used, the hours to be worked, and the supervisor to whom to report.

Job descriptions for maintenance personnel may be prepared by the personnel committee with the aid of the property management committee and members of the maintenance staff. Clear job descriptions help the prospective employee, the present staff, and the church members to know what each worker is expected to do.

Overlapping responsibilities and important gaps where no specific responsibility has been assigned are sometimes discovered in the process of preparing job descriptions. A basis for the equitable balancing of work assignments among employees is another benefit provided by job descriptions. They aid the employee and church leaders in evaluating the performance of the worker. Satisfactory performance of all items in the job description may properly become the basis for pay increases, for increased responsibility, and for available promotions.

Job responsibilities of some church employees may fluctuate from month to month. In such situations, the job description should be sufficiently broad and flexible to accommodate changes that may occur. A simple job description for a "one-man" maintenance staff might read as follows:

Church Janitor Job Description

Principal Function:
Keep physical property clean, comfortable, orderly, and in good operating condition.

Regular Duties:
1. Sweep, clean, and dust the offices daily.
2. Sweep, clean, and dust the nursery after each day of use.
3. Sweep, clean, and dust all other parts of the building according to schedule.
4. Scrub, wax, and polish all floors according to schedule or oftener as needed.
5. Clean all rest rooms and replenish all supplies daily.
6. Move tables, chairs, and other equipment as directed by supervisor.
7. Mow lawn, trim shrubbery, remove debris, and clean walks and parking areas as directed by supervisor.
8. Make minor repairs as needed.

Other Duties:
1. Wash walls and windows as requested.
2. Paint rooms as assigned.
3. Perform messenger service as requested by supervisor.
4. Perform other duties as assigned by supervisor.

The job description should be discussed at the time of employment and copies of it should be given to the employee, to his supervisor, and to the chairman of the property management committee.

In addition to the basic job description, supplementary instructions and requests should be passed along to the employee to keep him informed of changing needs and circumstances. These instructions should come to the employee through the supervisor indicated in the church organization chart.

DEVELOP A MANUAL OF OPERATIONS

Operation manuals for the guidance of employees, committees, and members of the staff are highly recommended. Such a manual should include an organization chart of the maintenance staff and a description of each maintenance job. It should also include regulations and procedures regarding the use of church property, the acquisition of supplies and equipment, and the adding or terminating of employees. Such a manual can be quite helpful in employee orientation and training. Morale goes up when people know the tasks they are expected to do, why they are doing them in a certain way, and that when they do them well their work will be appreciated.

SALARY SCALES

Beginning salaries for full-time maintenance personnel should be high enough to enable the employee to enjoy a comfortable standard of living. The prevailing wage scale of custodians and janitors in other agencies or institutions in the community should give an indication of a suitable wage for such work in the church. If the employee is able to perform many tasks that would otherwise require skilled workmen, his pay should reflect this added contribution to the welfare of the church. A maintenance man who can do routine electrical, plumbing, and carpentry work is valuable to the church.

Hours of work for full-time personnel should be consistent with community practice—usually a 40-hour week scheduled according to a pattern acceptable to the church. When overtime work is required—as may occur during special occasions such as weddings and conventions—additional remuneration should be provided.

FRINGE BENEFITS

Holidays to be given maintenance staff should be clearly stated in writing in the agreement worked out at the time of employment. Church programs may require maintenance employees to work on some days normally granted as holidays. Alternate holidays should be granted in such cases.

Vacations (usually two weeks with pay for all employees serving for at least one year) are customary. This gives the employee an opportunity to get away for a refreshing break from the routine of work and usually results in improved work, better morale, and a more cooperative spirit. Vacations can usually be scheduled several months in advance, during a period when church activities are at a minimum.

Sick leave that provides for five or more days of absence from work as needed should be included in the original work agreement. Without it an employee may report for work when he is sick, thus exposing others to his illness or further endangering his health and rapidity of recovery. Some churches base the number of permissible sick-leave days on the number of years of service.

Coffee breaks are now provided for most employees, usually fifteen minutes each morning and each afternoon.

Retirement plans are becoming standard practice for all church employees. Social Security is almost always provided for the maintenance staff and, in some cases, denominational retirement benefits are provided in whole or in part by the church.

Health and accident insurance is usually provided either wholly or in part by the church. Workmen's compensation insurance coverage is also provided by some churches for specified employees. Such coverage is mandatory under the laws of some states.

PERSONNEL COMMITTEE RESPONSIBILITIES

In most churches the personnel committee is the appropriate group to determine equitable salary and fringe benefits arrangements. It is the responsibility of this committee to study what is being paid in the community for the type of work to be done and what fringe benefits should be provided. It should recommend policies regarding employment procedures, including provision for merit increases, vacations, sick leave, insurance, and other personnel benefits.

How do salaries and fringe benefits of the church's employees compare with those provided by other churches in the same locality? Do they compare favorably with salaries and benefits of employees of schools, hospitals, and related agencies? The church personnel committee should make recommendations to the church governing body regarding needed changes in salaries and benefits.

In cooperation with the pastor and the property management committee, the personnel committee should prepare and distribute to all employees a written statement of policy and practice regarding salaries and benefits provided by the church. This written statement should be accompanied by oral explanations. Opportunity for questions and discussion should be given employees in order to facilitate thorough understanding of what benefits are provided, what limitations and conditions are involved, and what procedures the employee should follow to qualify for available benefits.

REGULATIONS CONCERNING TOOLS
AND EQUIPMENT

Churches usually purchase and retain ownership of the tools and equipment used in maintaining their property.

In some cases, maintenance employees bring to the job some of their own tools. This practice may create problems when employees leave the church and tools must be divided according to their proper ownership. About the only way to resolve this problem is to inventory and permanently mark all church-owned tools at the time of purchase. Employees should likewise mark the tools they bring to the church.

STRUCTURE THE WORK SCHEDULE

To plan a realistic schedule of work it is necessary to estimate the amount of time required to do each maintenance task satisfactorily. What is a "good day's work"? How many square feet of floor space should a man be able to clean in a day? How long should it take to wash the windows in a given building? How long should it require to dust and arrange furniture in a church classroom? These questions can and should be answered.

The supervisor, or the property management committee, in planning work schedules, should begin with standard figures and then make local adjustments in the light of the condition of the building, the amount of use various areas receive, and the amount of soil accumulation. Work schedules can help make sure that all essential operation and maintenance needs are being provided. They help balance the work load for all maintenance employees.

Several systems have been devised to provide standards of measurement for janitorial work. Probably the most widely used is based on a formula devised by F. LeRoy Gilbert. This formula resulted from time-study research which sought to identify the number of "work units" involved in cleaning a given room. In arriving at the number of "work units" to be assigned to each janitor, the formula adjusts the number of square feet per hour assigned. Consideration is given to such factors as the type of floor coverings and the number and kinds of doors, windows, light fixtures, partitions, equipment items, and furnishings to be cleaned in each area.

In using the Gilbert Formula, or adaptations of it, an inventory of each room is made, recording the number of square feet in the area, the type of floor covering, and the number of each item of furniture and equipment (chairs, pianos, tables). Each of these items is assigned an allotted number of "work units." The work load for a given room is calculated by multiplying each item by the number of "work units" assigned to it, then obtaining a total. In the Gilbert Formula a chair carries one work unit; a waste basket, two work units; a desk, three; a large table, two; a small table, one; a bookcase, one; a washbasin, two; and a windowsill, one. The total janitorial work load is determined by adding the work units for all areas, including hallways, rest rooms, walks, and parking areas. Each employee may be expected to care for about 250 work units per hour, according to the Gilbert Formula.

For churches desiring a simpler system, here are some suggestions. Begin by asking an experienced employee to keep a record of the jobs he does and the amount of time he spends on each job each day, for a period of at least two weeks. The amount of work being done, when compared with "standard norms," may indicate a need for evaluating the work procedures now being followed. Conferences with school executives and with appropriate officials of local churches regarding the work loads of their janitorial staffs should yield helpful comparative data. Although many church janitors perform numerous other duties, an average janitor should ordinarily be able to clean 1,000 square feet per hour in education space, 1,500 square feet per hour in auditoriums, and 2,000 square feet per hour in corridors.

By multiplying the time required for a single performance of each janitorial task by the number of times it must be done each week, one can determine the approximate number of hours of janitorial service needed per week, and thus the number of persons needed to get the work done.

Daily, weekly, and annual schedules of work should be prepared for each maintenance employee. They should list the basic tasks to be performed and should indicate where and when the work should be done. Good schedules of this kind not only serve as guides for maintenance employees but also enable the supervisor and others to know where each employee is supposed to be at any given time.

Supervisory personnel can use the work schedule in directing maintenance work and in evaluating individual performance. Employees can use it as a checklist of routine tasks to be performed. Schedules should indicate the frequency of maintenance operations in offices, auditoriums, nurseries, assembly rooms, classrooms, corridors, and toilets.

Members of the church congregation and leaders of other groups using church facilities should be informed regarding the proper channels for requesting maintenance services from the staff. By adopting specific policies and procedures, the church will likely secure a higher level of effectiveness in maintenance.

Chapter Summary

1. Descriptive job titles and clear job descriptions enable each employee to know what he is expected to do, when the work is to be done, and in what manner.

2. Job descriptions, employment policies, salary scales, and fringe benefits should be recommended by the personnel committee for consideration by the chief governing body of the church.

Chapter 4

TRAINING
AND SUPERVISING
CUSTODIAL STAFF

ACCOMPLISHING CHURCH OBJECTIVES and goals requires a spirit of teamwork that usually can be inspired through effective training and supervision of staff personnel. Workers find satisfaction in a job well done, in meaningful association with other staff members, and in rendering church-related services. These intrinsic values often carry greater weight than monetary remuneration or fringe benefits.

Staff training and supervision should be provided for all, whether employees or volunteers, who work at the job of maintaining church property. Results usually include improvement of skills, conservation of energy, better morale, and higher standards of work.

TRAINING FOR EFFECTIVE MAINTENANCE

A good training program can instill within the worker a sense of pride, importance, and meaningfulness of vocation. Training not only develops on-the-job skills, but also stimulates helpful attitudes toward work. Careful instruction, motivation, and appreciation of the worker are essential in bringing him to his full potential.

A letter of welcome from the pastor, or from some other member of the staff, should ordinarily be sent to each new employee. This letter should provide information about the church and its purposes and seek to enlist the new employee as a member of the team to help achieve the church's objectives. In an interview with the pastor, the new worker should be helped to understand his own contribution to the program of the church, procedures in staff relationships, policies that affect staff members, and means of self-improvement and advancement.

The next step in training the new employee should be his introduction to other staff members. If there are other maintenance workers, they should meet with the new employee and discuss the duties of all so that each may know what he and others are expected to do.

A tour of the church plant may be helpful in locating service areas, equipment rooms, and facilities for which the new employee will be responsible. He should be given a written job description and an understanding of the channels of written and oral communication. A bell or buzzer system can communicate emergency messages. By working out a code for different types of messages, time can be saved for both secretarial and maintenance staff.

ON-THE-JOB TRAINING

Training and supervision of maintenance workers should be continuous. Many employees can rise from mediocrity to real success through proper supervision and continual training. The best way to get more results for the money expended on maintenance is to provide adequate instruction of maintenance personnel. Increased productivity of the worker is the key to cost control in property maintenance. Wages absorb all but a few cents of each dollar allocated for cleaning. The cost of cleaning building space has increased tremendously. To keep this cost within reason, new time-saving equipment should be provided and the employee should be trained to use it efficiently and to keep it in good working order.

TRAINING IN THE USE OF MATERIALS
AND EQUIPMENT

Maintenance employees have frequently had little or no training or experience in such work. Most churches have only one custodial employee. The former custodian is seldom available to train the new employee. In some cases the pastor and the property management committee members may not feel qualified to provide the appropriate instruction. New employees are frequently obliged to learn the job by trial and error. Consequently, the workman may be dismissed and the same vicious cycle repeated.

The greater the turnover in maintenance personnel, the clearer it becomes that a training program is an urgent need. If new employees with little or no previous experience or training are assigned immediately to a job with inadequate supervision, they must learn by trial and error. They often adopt procedures that are not efficient and some of their errors may prove quite costly.

TYPES OF TRAINING

Training may be provided on a long-range apprenticeship basis when the church has a maintenance staff of two or more persons. A skilled employee can give instruction, observe the practices of the new employee, and continue to give guidance until the desired skills are mastered. A church may find it advisable to send a new employee to work in another church or institution for on-the-job training.

Employees should be given an opportunity to develop and apply new methods of work. Observing experienced workers moving efficiently through the various cleaning steps provides opportunities for acquiring know-how and self-assurance. Comparisons of old and new equipment and methods are helpful. For example, two classrooms of equal size might be cleaned, using a straw broom for one and a treated mop for the other. The typical lost motion of an inexperienced worker should be demonstrated in one room; the quick, purposeful motions of a trained cleaner should be used in the other. The ease and efficiency in using a cleaning cart with all supplies and equipment on hand could be demonstrated convincingly.

Group Discussion Sessions: Maintenance personnel from groups of churches might convene for study and conference. Such meetings could be arranged by councils of churches or by appropriate denominational leaders. Conference leaders could be enlisted from schools or from firms producing or distributing maintenance supplies.

A training program may be conducted by an expert maintenance employee of a church or a school, or by an instructor supplied by some janitorial supply company. A member of the church property management committee may be qualified to assume this responsibility. Films available from several companies show proper methods of using their products. Lectures, demonstrations, and informal conversation may accompany visits to other buildings for observation of proper maintenance procedures. Tours of church buildings can provide specific suggestions on jobs to be done, materials and methods to be used, and recommended procedures of performance.

A minimum training program provides on-the-job guidance of new employees until they learn how to perform acceptably the basic duties assigned. Instructions should be given in the use of equipment and supplies, the proper method for performing various tasks, the standard of cleanliness expected in each area, and the amount of time normally required for each phase of the job.

RESULTS OF EMPLOYEE TRAINING

Henry H. Linn suggests eleven results of an adequate training program.[1]

[1] Henry H. Linn, ed., *School Business Administration* (New York: The Ronald Press Company, Copyright © 1956), p. 401.

A properly conducted training program for employees should result in the following economies and improvements:

1. Higher standards of service.
2. Fewer employees needed because of increased efficiency of service production.
3. Less waste of materials used in custodial service.
4. Greater efficiency in boiler operation with less waste of fuel.
5. Less waste of electricity, gas, and water.
6. Reduction of fire and accident hazards.
7. Greater flexibility in shifting employees from one building to another.
8. Slower deterioration of plant and equipment.
9. More of the minor repairs to be cared for by the custodial personnel.
10. A more professional spirit among the employees.
11. A greater respect for custodial service and workers on the part of the general lay public.

TESTING AND INSPECTING

The evidence of effective training is improved performance. Training should include demonstrations followed by pertinent discussion and by utilization of a new procedure under supervision. Errors can be corrected and suggested work patterns established through this positive approach to testing and inspecting. Oral and written tests indicate the extent of factual information communicated.[2]

Maintenance workers should be encouraged to put into practice new and improved methods. Supervisory personnel should inspect the work, evaluate the results, and

[2] The Puritan Chemical Company, 916 Ashby Street, N.W., Atlanta 18, Georgia, has prepared helpful tests for use in training personnel. Answer sheets supplied give the correct answers and explain why this answer is important. The answer sheets contain some product promotion for the company but are quite valuable as a source of information for supervisor and employees.

commend the maintenance staff for improvements effected.

Maintenance personnel, whether the janitor in a one-room building or the air-conditioning engineer in a multi-million-dollar building, are all in the forefront of public relations for the church. It is extremely important that employees realize that they may maintain or destroy the church's good relations with its own members and with others who use or see its buildings and grounds. Employees should be trained not only in the proper performance of their maintenance duties but also in the fine art of getting along with people. Fortunate are they who feel that they are performing their task as a religious ministry as well as rendering faithful service for remuneration received.

The care and upkeep of church property is serious and significant work. It should not be attempted by incompetent persons employed through an act of charity. The expectations of church members concerning the cleanliness, orderliness, and safety of their church buildings and equipment demand that the best available personnel be sought and trained for this work.

ENCOURAGING SATISFACTORY PERFORMANCE

People work to satisfy their objectives. They have many kinds of objectives: satisfaction of hunger, attainment of financial security, acquisition of material possessions, and advancement to positions of power or prestige. To obtain satisfactory performance from its maintenance workers, the church must provide adequate opportunity for them to accomplish at least some of these objectives.

One extrinsic motivation is the desire for salary or wages. Wage scales should compare favorably with those of employees doing similar work elsewhere in the community.

The employee's work should be regularly supervised and inspected. He should be assured that faithful and effective performance will be rewarded with merit increases in salary. Upgrading the janitorial service should involve the use of better cleaning methods, better tools, better training, more careful scheduling. It should also include an incentive pay system to give proper reward for superior performance. Such merit increases should be given only after careful evaluation of regular inspection reports that indicate the performance level of the employee during the preceding work period.

Church employees have many would-be "bosses," some of whom occasionally seem to feel free to attempt to supervise custodial workers. The property management committee should clearly and publicly identify the responsible supervisor from whom maintenance workers are to receive instructions.

Maintenance employees should respond courteously and cheerfully to all requests. If they explain tactfully that they are instructed to channel all such requests to their supervisor, misunderstandings and complaints of church members who forget to convey their requests through appropriate channels will be minimized.

SUPERVISING THE MAINTENANCE STAFF

Supervision consists of building an effective work force and stimulating each member of it to perform at his best. Good supervisors get work done through others; they don't merely give orders or oversee employees to make sure that the rules are followed.

Observe a man attentive to his hobby. Notice the diligence, the enthusiasm, the vigor. Take a look at this same man at work for others. Does he manifest the same energy and enthusiasm as when working at his hobby? If not, it might be that he lacks motivation and training. A good supervisor seeks to provide employment conditions through which he can help each worker find means of self-expression, achievement, and individual development. Good supervisors maintain acceptable work standards, but they use their authority to enhance, rather than threaten, the worker's self-respect and personal integrity.

Maintenance personnel sometimes fail to produce satisfactorily because they lack constructive supervision. Those seeking guidance are frequently told that the pastor or supervisor knows even less about their work than they do. Accordingly, they must do the best they can. Probably the only communication with the custodial staff is to register complaints. If the building stays fairly comfortable and the dirt on the floors and dust on the furniture isn't too noticeable, the custodial staff may be left alone. If the supervisor is poorly informed and disinterested, the maintenance staff will function at the minimum level.

The need for adequate supervision poses a real problem for churches that are unable to retain the services of a business manager. This problem might be solved by naming to the property management committee members who have a knowledge of proper maintenance procedures—or a member of the ministerial staff might research this field until he is able to give adequate supervision. Experts from school maintenance staffs or building engineers from local businesses or industry may be employed on a consultant basis to inspect the church property each week and to give the maintenance staff guidance where needed.

Whichever route the church may take to provide supervision, routine inspection of all church property should be conducted regularly to ensure high standards of maintenance. When the employee knows that his work will be inspected by people who want to help him succeed, he will take greater interest and pride in his work. Employees should be encouraged to make notes of repairs and replacements that may need attention. When inspection reveals improper or substandard work, this should be tactfully discussed with the employee and suggestions made as to how the work may be done more satisfactorily. A checklist used during inspection helps the supervisor keep an accurate record of items needing attention.

STUDY PROCEDURES AND WORK STANDARDS

The supervisor helps each employee to use efficient work methods. He determines what motions are necessary to perform each task, what tools are needed, and what sequence of tasks can achieve the best results in the shortest time. If there are two or more maintenance employees, the supervisor makes an equitable distribution of the work load by dividing either the areas of responsibility or the type of work that they are to do. The supervisor should evaluate each employee's use of time—how many trips he makes for tools or supplies, how much actual productive work time is spent, delays experienced, interruptions, and other events affecting productivity.

A supervisor should expect of each employee a cooperative attitude, satisfactory performance, and a reasonable degree of aggressiveness and initiative. The employee in turn should receive direction and fair, consistent treatment from the supervisor, and an appreciation of the work being done. Just as every human being craves recognition and appreciation, so will each maintenance staff member appreciate the supervisor's sincere personal interest in him as a person.

The supervisor should know both the abilities and shortcomings of staff members, their likes and dislikes, their ambitions, their basic point of view in life. He should be quick to compliment the worker for a job well done; if there must be critical comment, let this be given privately.

COMMUNICATING WITH EMPLOYEES

Relations with the maintenance personnel can often be improved by the way in which instructions are communicated to them. Workers respond more readily when instructions are expressed as requests, such as "When you have time would you. . . . Would you . . . when you have finished this job?" This gives the employee an opportunity to raise questions freely without seeming to question a direct order. It helps the worker to know that his feelings, schedule, and plans are being considered.

When employees know why they are asked to do certain things, they do them more cheerfully. When the employee knows why certain equipment is being moved, why the nursery must be cleaned before a certain meeting, he is more likely to cooperate. Nothing is gained by keeping him in the dark about the basic objectives, programs, and activities of the church. Communication is furthered by providing the staff with church calendars of forthcoming activities and notifying them of any additions or changes. A copy of this calendar, with a weekly schedule of activities, should be prominently posted in the custodian's headquarters.

EMPLOYEE PERFORMANCE EVALUATION

Regular inspection of property maintenance by the designated supervisor is essential to superior performance. Such inspection should be followed by an expression of appreciation of work well done. A diligent workman deserves to have his efforts observed and appreciated. The supervisor of maintenance or members of the property management committee may use an inspection report form in monthly or quarterly evaluation of maintenance work. A suggested form is shown in Figure 3 on page 72.

Members of the property management committee and the maintenance staff should regularly tour the buildings to look for evidence of disorder and inadequate care. Such may include wilted floral arrangements or potted plants, pictures not hanging straight, accumulated periodicals and papers (many of them out of date and no longer used), dog-eared hymnals that need major repairs, or an indiscriminate mismatching of several varieties of chairs

Figure 3

Inspection Report Sheet

(To be Used by Property Management Committee)

A.M.

Date_____Time_____P.M.   Inspected by_____

(Indicate condition by writing in clean, dirty, good, bad, broken, etc.)

Room	Floor	Walls	Ceiling	Woodwork	Windows	Plumbing	Hardware	Lights	Rema

Recommendations:

Signed _____

in the same room. If one could imagine himself a guest visiting another church, what impressions, favorable and unfavorable, would one likely gain from seeing property in the condition of his own? Would the grounds, the entrance, the building, and the arrangement of furnishings and equipment create a sense of beauty, cleanliness, warmth, and welcome?

CAUSES OF POOR PERFORMANCE

What are the most frequent causes of poor performance by maintenance personnel? Experience varies, but frequently the following are involved:

1. Poor communication and interpersonal relations
2. Lack of ability or unwillingness to develop skills
3. Lack of clear job description
4. Inadequate supervision
5. Too many "bosses"

6. Emotional immaturity or insecurity
7. Off-the-job difficulties
8. Poor health

By being aware of these difficulties, church leaders can be alert to indications of their presence in prospective employees and, when discovered among those who are employed, can take corrective measures.

MAINTENANCE COST CONTROLS

One of the responsibilities of the supervisor of maintenance is the control of maintenance costs. He will also need to be able to estimate these costs for the budget-planning committee, so that he will be assured of adequate resources for maintenance.

A church should expect to spend about 15 percent of its annual budget on maintenance. This would include the cost of janitorial and other maintenance salaries, janitorial supplies, utilities, and the cost of routine repairs and upkeep. Major repairs and remodeling would be added to these amounts. If corrective and preventive maintenance have been neglected, emergencies involving major expenditures may be expected at any time. The age, general condition of the property, local conditions affecting property deterioration, and the quality of maintenance in previous years will all affect the maintenance costs. Budgetary allocation of one percent of what it would cost to replace the building is suggested as a minimum expected cost for routine repairs and upkeep. Another two percent of the replacement cost is suggested for property operation, cleaning, and other housekeeping expenses.

Average expected costs for various aspects of maintaining church buildings are shown on the chart in Figure 4.

KEEP ADEQUATE RECORDS

Adequate records are essential to budgeting, purchasing, and inventory control. Records should be kept of all pur-

Figure 4

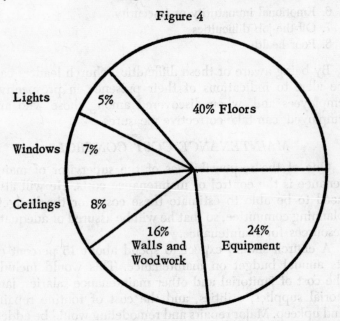

Lights 5%

40% Floors

Windows 7%

Ceilings 8%

16% Walls and Woodwork

24% Equipment

Labor costs for the care of floors, cleaning and replacement of lights, cleaning and weatherproofing of windows and doors, cleaning and other routine care of ceilings, walls and woodwork, the operation of the heating and cooling equipment, and care of the grounds will absorb over 75 percent of the maintenance budget in most churches.

chases for building operation and maintenance, indicating date of order and delivery, seller, price, and amount of material or services obtained. Inventory of janitorial supplies and equipment should be a matter of record so that reorders can be placed in time to have supplies when needed. Records should also be kept of repairs, painting, waxing, and operations such as servicing heating and air-conditioning equipment, fire extinguishers, musical instruments, and office equipment. Inspections should record on the checklists items that need attention. Dates of completion of work on these items should be shown on the record forms. If mechanical equipment, musical instruments, or the roof is under warranty, it is important that complete records be kept of all service and maintenance operations in order to substantiate any claims that may need to be made under the warranty, as well as to insure proper routine care.

PURCHASING POINTERS

Maintenance equipment and supplies should be purchased from reputable dealers offering prompt service and replacement parts. The church should have one central purchasing procedure to facilitate quantity buying, budget control, and supervision. Consult with public school officials or some of the larger industries in the area regarding the best sources of dependable janitorial supplies. Do not buy an expensive commercial cleaner when a simple homemade solution will serve the same purpose just as well. Ammonia in water makes a good window cleaner. Inexpensive tri-sodium phosphate makes a good general cleaner. For equipment purchases and contract work, secure bids with written specifications and performance guarantees. Ask for a demonstration of any new product being promoted. Store materials as near the point of use as possible.

A PLACE FOR EVERYTHING

Every church should have one central custodial headquarters at which should be kept blueprints of the building, an inventory of equipment, and careful records of any changes made in the construction of the buildings such as the laying of new sewer or water lines or changes in the electrical circuits. All documents giving instructions for the operation of equipment, and guarantees and service warranties should be kept in a central office, available to all who need to see them, yet not allowed to get scattered and lost. Manufacturers will supply a second manual of instructions for the master file, to supplement the copy given to the maintenance personnel.

In the small church building, a single closet may be the only available location for custodial maintenance equipment and supplies. The need for adequate space for storage of such items should not be overlooked in the construction or remodeling of church buildings. In multi-story buildings or separate buildings, service rooms or closets for janitor's equipment and supplies are needed on each floor.

If the maintenance program is to be successful, the employee must take pride in his work. If he is expected to keep all the building clean, orderly, and attractive, he should have headquarters and storage space that can be kept clean and orderly. A dingy corner under a stairway, lacking sufficient room to store equipment and supplies, will discourage and handicap a potentially capable worker.

EVERYTHING IN ITS PLACE

A room or closet, centrally located on each floor, for the exclusive use of the maintenance staff in storage of cleaning supplies and equipment will save labor costs by preventing loss of time in gathering supplies and equipment. (More time is lost due to employees going back and forth between the source of their supplies and tools and their place of work than for any other reason.) A cleaning cart that, mounted on casters, carries all the supplies and equipment needed in cleaning rooms on that floor, and a container for trash, will prove to be a time-saver for the cleaning staff. The minimum size recommended for a janitor's closet is thirty-five square feet. It should provide adequate sources of both hot and cold water for custodial use. Floor drains with an 8-inch curbing or deep utility sinks at floor level are better than utility sinks at the usual level. Such an arrangement facilitates the use of mopping equipment that can be drained easily and refilled with clean water quickly and conveniently. Adequate shelving and equipment hooks will help keep supplies and equipment in order and in place. Maintenance headquarters should be equipped with a workbench and tools for repair work. Lockers and washroom facilities for maintenance employees should be provided.

Employees should notify the supervisor whenever supplies are running low and need to be reordered, or when equipment needs to be replaced.

By placing the following items on the cleaning cart, return trips for tools and supplies can be reduced or eliminated:

trash sack	putty knife
mop bucket and wet mop	pliers
treated dry mop for floor	screwdriver
sweeping	toilet-bowl brush
floor brush	rubber gloves
counter brush	paper towels and toilet paper
wall brush	cleaning solutions
dustcloth	report pad to note needed
scrub rag	maintenance
dustpan	

Chapter Summary

1. Every church should designate an individual, a staff member or the chairman of the property management committee, to supervise the maintenance program.

2. The designated supervisor should conduct a routine inspection of all church property at least weekly to determine whether adopted standards are maintained.

3. Performance of maintenance employees should be evaluated periodically and continuously.

4. Staff training can upgrade the level of maintenance through introduction of improved materials and techniques.

Chapter 5

INSPECTING AND INVENTORYING PROPERTY

EFFECTIVE MAINTENANCE of church property begins with a thorough inspection and a complete inventory. All church-owned buildings and equipment should be included: each room, hall, stairway, attic, and basement; the roof, the walls, and the foundation; the walks, driveways, parking areas, and landscaping. A list should be made of all equipment and furniture, whether in use or in storage. A number to provide permanent identification should be either glued or painted on each item. A list should indicate the items assigned to each room.

The initial inspection and inventory should be followed by a regular schedule of subsequent inspections, using checklists to be sure all items are accounted for and are in proper condition. Any changes in the use of space or equipment call for special inspections and possible reassignment of furnishings. In the event of storm damage, vandalism, or other unusual circumstances, a special inspection may be needed to determine the full extent of the loss. The accuracy of the claim will largely depend on the reliability and adequacy of inspection and inventory records. Before paying any claims, insurance companies often require a complete room list of items damaged or destroyed. A master list should therefore be kept in a fire-proof location outside the church building.

THE INITIAL INSPECTION

The seriously ill person needs the best available physician to diagnose his case. Amateur opinions and recommendations can be dangerous. Likewise, a building that has a serious physical problem needs the attention of expert diagnosticians who can discover its weaknesses and help to preserve its strengths. A capable architect is one kind of specialist that may be needed in a complete building inspection. An experienced engineer, general or mechanical contractor, electrical, plumbing, or heating and air-conditioning expert may be requested to aid in making the inspection. They may be accompanied by the pastor and a member of the church maintenance staff who can give information about difficulties and other malfunctions encountered in the buildings and equipment. The checklist used in the initial inspection may be used also in subsequent inspections. It should include the following items.[1]

ROOFS

A defective roof can cause a multitude of maintenance problems. It can cause rotting and collapse of trusses supporting the roof. It can cause deterioration of plaster, wood, paint, floor coverings, and furnishings. One of the most important functions of the maintenance staff is to prevent the roof from leaking.

Since roofs are difficult and expensive to repair, it is important to use the most dependable and durable material that the church can afford when constructing or re-

[1] Inspection and Repair Procedures adapted from "The High Cost of Neglect" by Herbert W. Holgren and H. J. Campbell, Jr., in *Protestant Church Building Administration Equipment*, February, 1957, pp. 18ff. Used by permission.

building a roof. Lasting qualities of any roof are determined by its ability to resist the action of the elements—wind, water, snow and freezing rain, gaseous fumes, soot, and climatic changes with resultant expansion and contraction. Fire resistance of any roof is particularly important. The ideal roofing would require no additional treatment such as paint or coating with other material for its preservation and its satisfactory performance. Nails, screws, clips, adhesive, or other fastenings used to hold the roof in place should ideally last as long as the roofing material itself.

Built-up Roofs: Built-up roofs consist of layers of saturated felt mopped with hot pitch or bitumen, with slag or crushed stone on top. Remove a small section of slag to examine the membrane. Look for cracks, punctures or evidence of water between layers of felt. If felt is sound but has a dry, lifeless appearance, all gravel should be removed and sifted to remove dirt. The entire surface should then be mopped with a hot surfacer, and the gravel (slag or stone) replaced. If the roof is fifteen to twenty years old, a new roof surface may be in order.

Sloping Roofs: Defects may be found by looking in the attic for evidence of leaks. Sloping roofs may be constructed with many coverings. Wood shingles should not be considered by churches because of their lack of fire resistance. Asbestos shingles are not likely to prove satisfactory because of breakage and high maintenance costs. Asphalt shingles, if heavy enough and properly manufactured, may give many years of service. Tile roofs in certain areas are quite popular but for satisfactory service depend on a sound and enduring under layer of waterproof membrane. A copper roof is practically maintenance-free. It does not require painting and is little affected by corrosive chemicals in the atmosphere. Slate roofing for churches continues to be popular. It can be obtained in varying colors and, when properly installed, gives many years of service. In time slates tend to become loosened by wind, by rusting away of original fasteners, and by freezing and thawing. As they slide down from their original location, they often cut open gutters and cornices, creating serious water problems in the walls beneath.

OTHER PROBLEM AREAS

Copings: Most older buildings with flat roofs have a coping (low parapet wall). This parapet is the origin of many leaks. Examine the coping stones or tiles at the top of the wall. Make sure that none is loose or missing and that the joints between the stones are tight and well pointed to prevent water seeping down walls and entering ceiling spaces. Examine inside face of wall for open mortar joints or soft and porous bricks that allow water to infiltrate. Replace all missing or defective coping stones. Point up all open mortar joints. If brick work on roof side of wall is in bad condition, apply a coat of cement mortar from top of flashings to underside of coping.

Flashing: The juncture between membrane roofing and parapet wall is generally metal, usually copper. Make sure that flashings are intact and free from punctures.

Roof Drains, Gutters, and Leaders: Make sure that drains are free from debris and fitted with strainers. If leaders run on outside walls, inspect for rust holes or breaks. Ice forming inside will crack or deform them. Make certain that all leaders, gutters, and flashings are watertight.

Ironwork on Roof: Inspect all metal scuttles, skylights, bulkhead doors, and tank supports for peeling paint and rusting. Have all defective surfaces scraped or wire-brushed and repainted. Use one coat of red lead, or iron oxide paint, and one coat of lead and oil paint.

Masonry: Examine all brick surfaces and mortar joints carefully. Brickwork on different surfaces of the same building will vary from good to bad due to different exposure to the elements. Examine for settlement cracks. A slight initial settlement often occurs in wall-bearing construction, resulting in small cracks generally found alongside of windows. Where brick arches occur over openings, check to see whether the bricks have slipped. Look for stains or damp spots due to faulty gutters or leaders, or defective joints in cornices or overhangs. Rake out loose mortar and point up all defective joints of brick or stone with cement mortar. If inside walls continue to be damp or if settlement cracks open up after painting, obtain professional advice as to the cause and remedy.

Painted Areas: Look for cracked and peeled paint or bare spots. Check for loose or missing caulking around windows and for cracked window glass and defective weather stripping. See whether windowsills need touch-up jobs between regular painting cycles. Check all fire escapes for rust and loose or missing bolts or parts, especially counterbalanced stairs or ladders. Check all railings, window guards, and miscellaneous metal. Wire-brush all wood surfaces to remove loose or scaled paint. Re-putty, and caulk as required and apply two coats of outside paint. Wire-brush ironwork to remove scale. Touch up rust or bare spots with red lead. Apply one or two coats of outside paint.

HAZARD AREAS

Regular periodic inspections should be made of all spaces, especially seldom-seen spaces, such as cellars, attics, towers, unused coal bunkers, and storage spaces. Look for fire hazards such as loose paper, paint cans, and oil rags in closets, under stairs, and in heater room. Look for obstructions of exit passages, doorways and fire escapes. Examine hardware of emergency exits to see that doors are operable. Check all room surfaces (walls, ceilings, windows, floors) and furnishings for cleanliness and needed repair, painting, and resurfacing. Install lighting, new equipment, and furniture needed to make rooms attractive, sanitary, and properly heated and ventilated. Check all floors for slipping, tripping hazards, and worn surfaces.

Basement: Remove all rubbish. Check wood beams, sills, wainscoting, cupboards, and closets for termites, dampness, and rot.

Kitchen and Toilets: The finish on all surfaces should ensure good sanitation. Check equipment against leaks and deterioration from rust and neglect. Be sure ventilation is adequate.

Windows and Doors: Replace cracked or broken glass and frayed or broken sash cords. Seal cracks around doors and windows with caulking compound. Repair loose or broken door locks, hinges, closers. Check for any repainting needed.

MECHANICAL AND ELECTRICAL MAINTENANCE

Mechanical and electrical systems should be inspected at least every six months by persons other than members of the regular maintenance staff. The inspecting team should be provided with a standard form checklist and should make its report in writing. The form should include the date, recommendations, and signatures of the inspectors.

Piping: Check insulation. Is insulation intact, and are bands and covering secure?

Are elbows and fittings properly packed?

Check all pipe hangers. Poorly hung pipe will develop leaks. Be sure that all hangers support pipes firmly and that bolts or clips are in place.

Check for leaks. Look for discoloration of insulation, excessive rusting or corrosion around pipe joints, oil film on oil piping, wet spots on floors and around valve handles. Check particularly inside radiator, convector, or equipment enclosures, and other connections to equipment.

Plumbing Fixtures: Chipped, broken, or cracked fixtures can be a health menace. Check all toilet fixtures.

Check faucets to prevent deterioration of fixtures. Check water closets and flush-tank mechanism, including bulb reseating, to ensure that water shuts off properly.

Check wall-hung fixtures, particularly lavatories, to be sure they are secure.

Check all water-closet seat hinges for tightness to prevent breakage and injury to children. This is a frequent cause of fixture breakage and may cause injury to small children.

Boiler Room: Check boiler and equipment rooms against fire hazard caused by storage of any kind.

Check for leaks evidenced by rust or corrosion on fittings and equipment, dampness on floor, or oil spots around burner. Special attention should be given to gauge glass (steam boiler), manifolds (cast-iron boiler), and all other equipment connections.

Duct Work: Check hangers and bracing to be certain support is adequate. Check leaks indicated by signs of dirt on ducts. Insulation should remain tight and form continuous seal along length. Inspect flexible connectors for tightness against rot and for easily cracked brittle connections.

Electrical Work: Check fixtures for cleanliness and physical condition. Dirty or broken fixtures can steal 50 to 70 percent of light output.

Check fuses for correct size. Fuse sizes should be painted on inside cover of switches and panels. Oversized fuses are never the answer to fuse blowing. It may be better to replace fuses with circuit breakers.

Check panel boards. All wiring should be concealed behind door trim enclosing panel. No loose wires should be permitted. All panel boards should have a directory indicating fuse or circuit breaker controls for each circuit.

Check for broken or loose receptacles and other outlets.

Check operation of all signal, public address, and inter-communication systems. Check operation of dimming equipment.

Check to insure that all wiring is complete, that conduit or cable is secured to boxes, and that covers are on all boxes.

Make sure electric system is not overloaded, wiring is not obsolete.

WATER, HEATING, ELECTRIC SYSTEMS

Oil and grease all motors, where required, at least every six months. Check belt tensions, condition and alignment of pulleys, and alignment and tightness of couplings. Oil or gas burner should be thoroughly cleaned at least once a year.

Clean flue and breeching once a year. Inspect flue (with a mirror) for cleanliness, tightness, and cracks.

See that boiler and burner are cleaned and vacuumed or blown out to remove soot as required—probably once each year.

Inspect condition of combustion chamber for loose bricks or cracks.

Every two years pump out fuel-oil tank to remove sludge, dirt, and water from bottom of tank in which heavy (Number 5 or 6) oil is used, and every three or four years if Number 2 is used.

Drain water from bottom of boiler to remove sludge. If there are two mud drums at bottom, drain each separately until water is clear. Check with other local operators to see if water requires treatment to prevent scaling (particularly for steam boilers). Check and clean steam boiler gauge glass and blow out any dirt. This should be done every six months, or more often, depending upon local water.

Check for system leaks at least once a year where much

piping is enclosed underground. Shut off makeup water feed and operate plant, under direct supervision, for eight hours. Any significant lowering of normal pressure in hot water system, or boiler water level in steam system, should be investigated.

At least once a year check all operation on *all* controls, particularly boiler controls, that is, combustion safety, pressure, switches, aquastats, low-water cutoffs, automatic boiler water feed. Check all relief valves every year. Flush out dirt or rust. See that all valves release and that settings are correct.

Check steam systems at least every two years—where areas receive very high usage, every year. Clean all strainers and traps to remove scale and other impurities. Check operation of air vents. If condensate or vacuum pump set is used, check complete operation.

Hot water systems should be checked every year. Inspect the expansion tank for proper air-water ratio. Check air vents to ensure proper functioning.

Check and vacuum convectors and radiators at least once a year. Close and open each water valve completely at least once a year, and note whether there is any leak. After valve has been turned to full-open position, turn one-half turn toward closed position. Tighten packing nut or repack if leaking.

Drain water off bottom of domestic water tank once a year to remove scale.

Check all air filters. Any fan or blower filter requires replacement every two to six months, depending upon usage and location. Permanent types require cleaning and replacement of adhesive on same schedule. Grease filters in kitchens require special attention because of fire hazard.

Ducts, Louvers, Grilles, Registers: Once a year clean outside air intakes and screens and inside grilles, registers, and ceiling diffusers. Excessive dirt indicates need for vacuuming duct work.

EQUIPMENT SERVICE RECORD

As the inventory is being made, a list of all mechanical equipment needing service should be accumulated. Service record cards should then be prepared for each of these items. Equipment requiring service includes electrical appliances, sound systems, projectors, heating and air-conditioning equipment, office equipment, recreational equipment, and furniture items such as pews, lecterns, tables, and chairs. The equipment service records should be kept in the general church office or in the headquarters of the maintenance staff, where they are readily available.

INSPECT NEW BUILDINGS

Before final acceptance of a new building from the contractor, it should be completely inspected. A checklist for each room should indicate the type of floor, type and color of paint, and a description of each item of equipment, including the name of its manufacturer and supplier, the location of the manual for its operation, and the manufacturers' warranties and service contracts, if any.

The architect and contractors should furnish the church with accurate blueprints and specifications corrected to show any changes made in the actual construction. Subsequent changes should be noted on the master copy of the blueprints kept by the church.

Furnishings List for New Building: In preparing to occupy a new building, or in moving classes or departments to a new location within present buildings, a complete list of all furnishings and equipment to be placed in each room should be prepared. If possible, old equipment should be refinished and repaired, if needed, before being moved into the new location. Pews, chairs and tables in any room should be of uniform design and color. Colors in floor coverings, walls, ceilings, and furniture should complement each other.

DETERMINING MAINTENANCE PRIORITIES

A complete inspection of a church building may reveal the need for numerous repairs. A leaking roof, a faulty furnace, a broken stair rail calls for and deserves immediate attention. Other repairs can and should be scheduled so as to give priority to the most essential work. Major maintenance repairs and replacements should be timed so as to make the best use of the skills and time of the regular maintenance employees, unless such work is done by contract.

PREVENTIVE MAINTENANCE

Prepare a master list of all maintenance tasks and repair work to be done. Assign to each job a tentative starting date and completion date and make an estimate of the total man-hours required to complete the job. Indicate which member or members of the maintenance staff is to perform the work or if it is to be done by outside contractors. Examine inspection checklists to be sure all needed repairs are included in the schedule.

Preventive maintenance reduces costs. Performed on a planned schedule, such operations as painting, re-roofing, and tuckpointing of brick or stone, keep the church buildings in sound condition and prevent costly deterioration. By servicing or replacing equipment on a schedule recommended by the manufacturer, damaging breakdowns can often be avoided. Preventive maintenance involves the immediate repair of minor items. Tightening a loose screw will often prevent damage to door or window hardware. Leaky faucets can be quickly repaired in most cases by replacing a faucet washer. Commodes not flushing properly can be unclogged before embarrassing overflows occur. Removal of debris from drains, gutters, and downspouts prevents serious water damage. When the janitorial staff carry along on the cleaning carts a pair of pliers, a screwdriver, an oil can, a putty knife and faucet washers, they can perform quickly many preventive maintenance operations.

MAINTENANCE BY STAFF OR CONTRACT

In some communities a church may be able to secure maintenance service of a higher quality and at a lower over-all cost by negotiating maintenance contracts with competent and dependable firms. Many churches have contracts for tuning and otherwise maintaining organs and pianos. Economical service contracts may be available for the service of office equipment. Churches may find it less expensive to hire outside contractors than to use and equip their own staffs for cleaning high ceilings and tall windows and replacing and repairing electrical fixtures in relatively inaccessible areas.

Contract workers are generally more skilled in their specialty than are the regular church maintenance employees. Contract maintenance firms have the tools and materials to do the work properly. Consequently, contract maintenance in whole or in part may prove more satisfactory than the use of church employees. If it is possible, however, to employ skilled maintenance workers on the church staff, they can be used effectively and economically because they are better acquainted with the buildings and the schedule of activities that should be permitted to go on as far as possible during maintenance and repair operations. The property management committee should examine each major maintenance project and decide on the basis of the available skills, tools, and materials whether the work should be done by the regular staff or an outside contractor.

Chapter Summary

1. Good maintenance of church property begins with a thorough inspection and a complete inventory of buildings and equipment.

2. Preventive maintenance is the best approach to keeping property in good condition.

3. Churches sometimes find it economical to contract with outside firms for part or all of their maintenance services.

CLEANING PROCEDURES

OBJECTIVES AND STANDARDS

THE PURPOSE of property maintenance is to aid the church in achieving its objectives. The objectives determine the standards for cleaning and custodial care. The maintenance program seeks to insure maximum comfort, convenience, and service. Those who use church property should endeavor to help the staff eliminate waste and correct conditions causing damage to buildings and equipment.

Both the small, compact church building and the majestic cathedral can be made more attractive, worshipful, and usable by proper cleaning and good housekeeping. Clean, orderly buildings silently invite guests to return. Untidy church buildings and grounds repel people and create a poor image of the church. The condition of church buildings communicates a message. Clean, attractive, well-ordered buildings bear silent witness to the importance that church members attach to their church. Proper care contributes greatly to favorable public relations in respect to both the general public and those in the church. Poorly kept buildings reflect congregational indifference and unconcern. It is difficult to create a favorable climate for learning or worship in a building with dusty pews, disordered chairs, and unsanitary surroundings. Buildings that are neat and clean engender respect and pride and discourage vandalism and abuse.

HEALTH FACTORS

Proper cleaning and custodial care will guard the health and safety of all those using the church buildings. Ministering to all age groups from toddlers to octogenarians, it is essential that the church custodial staff be concerned for the health and safety of all. Good maintenance will minimize instances of: underheating, overheating, poor ventilation, inadequate sanitation, improper lighting, unsatisfactory light control, uncontrolled noises, improper humidification, and recirculation of dust-laden air.

COOPERATION ESSENTIAL

Keeping the church buildings clean should be a cooperative endeavor. Although the maintenance staff is primarily responsible, the objective of clean, attractive facilities calls for cooperation of all who use the building. By their example and encouragement, church leaders can help keep equipment, furnishings, hymnbooks, pictures, and other supplies in good order. Cleaning up after education and recreation activities can be a helpful part of the learning experience for those participating. It can certainly greatly reduce the work load of maintenance employees.

Clean church buildings, properly arranged equipment, attractively painted walls and doors and well-kept lawns are not accidental. If church objectives are to be achieved, if the greatest number of people are to be reached and served, church-wide cooperative attention must be given to the cleaning of church facilities.

TIME FOR HOUSECLEANING?

Before discussing routine cleaning it should be pointed out that most churches need a major ruthless housecleaning that will remove loads of accumulated articles that are no longer used or not used often enough to justify the storage space the church has too long provided. Included are broken or discarded chairs, pews, and tables, and obsolete literature, discarded hymnbooks, other assorted castoffs, and accumulated trash.

Closets and storage areas should be specifically assigned for particular purposes and so used. Such a policy prevents any area from becoming a catchall for useless junk that defies good housekeeping and may become a fire hazard.

INSPECT AND REPAIR

The maintenance workers should be constantly alert to the need for repairs as they go about routine cleaning duties. Minor repairs can usually be made after their routine cleaning schedule is completed. In some cases, the repairs must be made before the cleaning of a given area. A clogged drain in a toilet fixture will require immediate attention and should be attended to before the rest room is cleaned.

Leaking valves, broken glass or latches on windows or doors, burned-out light bulbs, faulty switches, and other such items should be noted and repaired as regular work items on the daily schedule. Major repairs may require immediate action by church officials and outside repairmen to meet such emergencies as a breakdown of the heating plant or the electrical system or a storm-damaged roof. The malfunctioning of the heating or air-conditioning equipment, or leaks in the plumbing or roof, should be brought to the attention of the proper church authorities so that immediate steps can be taken to remedy the problem and prevent further damage.

PREVENTING DIRT ACCUMULATION

Cleaning is designed not only to remove dirt but, as far as possible, to prevent dirt from accumulating. Dirt may be airborne, may be brought in on shoes and clothing, or may be generated within the building.

Shoes dampened by rain or dew can accumulate sand or other gritty soil from walks, driveways, or parking areas. These abrasive substances cut through the wax finish on polished floors. Parking areas and walks should be surfaced with materials that will not damage floors. Great care should be given to provide means of preventing tracking in of dirt that damages and soils floors and that must be removed in the cleaning process. Walks should be laid out and shrubs planted in such a way as to discourage shortcuts through mud, wet grass, sand, dust, or dirt. Oil, grease, or tar accumulations on parking areas or driveways should be removed. Mats at entrances would enable persons to wipe off dust and mud before entering the building. On rainy days or when snow has fallen, long rubber mats may be unrolled in the halls inside each doorway to protect the floors.

PLANNING LOW-MAINTENANCE BUILDINGS

The choice of building materials used in constructing or remodeling a church building can affect considerably the cost of maintenance. Cleaning time and expense is determined by the kind of surfaces to be cleaned and the amount and kind of soil or dirt accumulating on those surfaces. It is a wise building committee that takes into consideration the cleaning and maintenance costs in planning a church building. The first cost at the time of construction too often determines the materials to be used. A realistic calculation of the maintenance costs over a 10- to 20-year period might indicate the wisdom and economy of choosing building materials requiring minimum maintenance.

Surfaces of polished stone, ceramic tile, glass, glazed brick, stainless steel, aluminum, and some plastics may be much more easily cleaned than those of porous wood, brick, or stone. Some materials are inherently freer of corrosion and are less likely to disintegrate. The use of surfaces that by their density or smoothness naturally resist the penetration or adhesion of various forms of soil reduces the cleaning costs.

SWEEPING AND CLEANING FLOORS

About 40 percent of the cost of custodial cleaning is applied to cleaning floors. Foot traffic and airborne dust deposit more soil on the floors than anywhere else. Floor coverings should be chosen in the light of the amount of traffic, the use that will be made of the area, their appearance, and their ease of maintenance. Many churches claim to have lowered maintenance costs by using carpeting in classrooms, assembly rooms, offices, hallways, and the sanctuary. In uncarpeted areas, floors will give better service and can be much more easily cleaned if they are given a protective coating of sealer and wax. Floors treated in this way will retain their attractive appearance and make the removal of soil much easier. Recommended procedures are indicated in the following chapter.

Different types of floor covering require different methods of cleaning. The custodial staff will be aided by a chart that indicates the types of flooring in each area and the approved cleaning methods. Sanitary supply houses will frequently provide manuals giving detailed suggestions on cleaning procedures.

The frequency of cleaning depends on the amount of use an area is given. Areas used daily, such as offices, need daily cleaning. Nurseries, kindergarten areas, kitchen, and food-service facilities need careful cleaning after each use. The church staff should advise the custodial personnel of times when various areas will be in use so that a suitable cleaning schedule can be maintained and the space will be ready for use as needed.

PROPER EQUIPMENT ESSENTIAL

Effective jobs of cleaning require appropriate equipment and supplies. Modern cleaning methods are far ahead of the old straw broom and feather duster. More efficient cleaning tools, such as electrically powered floor machines, vacuum cleaners that will pick up mop and rinse water as well as dry soil, and chemically treated dust mops and floor brushes, now make it possible for janitorial workers to do a much more thorough and more rapid job of cleaning.

All of the cleaning equipment needed to completely clean rooms on a given floor should be moved to the room on a portable cleaning cart. This cart should be equipped with a trash sack or container. No trips back to supply closets, garbage disposal or water and drain locations are needed if the cleaning cart is properly equipped. In unplanned and poorly equipped cleaning operations, as much as 40 percent of the employee's time can be spent on getting ready and in getting the tools, emptying waste baskets, filling or draining mop buckets.

A vacuum cleaner removes more than 50 percent more dirt than floor brushes or mops. In rooms with rough floors, or where there are heavy deposits of litter, trash, and soil on the floors, it is appropriate to use a floor brush and dustpan. Floor brushes made of horsehair, bristle, or nylon are much more satisfactory than straw brooms. Sweeping with a straw broom often merely scatters the dust. It does not produce the controlled sweeping job that is desirable. On most noncarpeted areas a chemically treated floor mop (three or four feet wide if furniture arrangements permit) will give better results than floor brushes or brooms. Such treated mops remove the dirt and polish the floor at the same time. The strands of the mop can whip around the legs of chairs and tables as brushes cannot do. Brushes and brooms require a series of stroking motions involving greater effort and time than does the steady pushing of a mop over the floor. These chemically treated mops must be frequently cleaned, however, to remove the soil that adheres to them. After laundering they should be re-treated with the required chemical solution, then rolled up for several hours before use, so that the chemical can permeate all the mop fibers. This treatment is much to be preferred over sweeping compounds sometimes used in sweeping wood floors. Oil-base sweeping compounds may cause deterioration of asphalt-tile floors, and should be used with care, if used at all.

STEPS IN CLEANING

Routine cleaning of a typical room should involve the following procedure: leaving the cleaning cart at the door, the janitor arranges furniture for cleaning, adjusts window shades, empties waste baskets into trash sack on cleaning cart and returns to the room with vacuum, mop, or floor brush for sweeping. If a dust mop is used, it should not be raised from the floor except at the end of the room near the door, from which point the dirt can be swept into the hall. The dust mop should be shaken, and the accumulated dirt from the room and the mop should be picked up with a dustpan and floor brush and placed in the dust box on the cleaning cart.

Dusting: Regular dusting should include all horizontal surfaces. Equipment may include attachments for the vacuum cleaner, so that it can be used to clean the area to be dusted. A long-handled wall brush should be available to clear cobwebs and dust from walls and ceiling. Soft, clean, dustcloths should be carried on the cart to complete the dusting process. This procedure of sweeping and dusting should be performed each week or more frequently if rooms are used more often.

Washing: At least once a month, the light fixtures should be wiped free of dust. To secure the maximum amount of light, the fixtures should be washed clean every three to six months. Accumulated dirt can reduce by as much as 50 percent the amount of light a fixture produced when new. Some plastics used in louvers and in other parts of lighting fixtures may develop charges of static electricity that will attract dust. If this is a problem, secure a special solution from a sanitary supply house that will counteract this effect when applied to the plastic material.

Some church buildings include large areas of glass. Glass doors need to be cleaned after each use of the building. Windows need cleaning at least once every three months in most communities. Materials containing abrasives or compounds that might scrape or dull the surface should not be used in cleaning stained glass. The lead frames often used in constructing stained glass windows can become quite brittle. They should be handled with great care when such windows are being cleaned. Ordinary glass windows may be washed with a sponge or soft cloth, using a commercial solvent in the wash water. Ammonia, alcohol, or vinegar solutions are frequently used. A window brush and squeegee may be used. Such tools are sometimes a bit awkward to use with small windows and may result in water damage on the floors and walls when used inside of the room. Commercial solvents sprayed on, then wiped off with a soft cloth, give good results.

In washing a window, begin at the upper left corner of the windowpane and move to the right with the sponge, brush, or cloth. Upon reaching the right side, with the sponge still in contact with the glass pane, move down and then back to the left across the pane. Continue the process from side to side in one continuous motion. When the bottom of the window is reached, reverse or clean the sponge. Beginning at the lower left corner, move up to the top then back down, until the entire window area has been covered a second time. Using a single stroke reduces fatigue and fosters greater speed and efficiency. This method is much less time consuming and more effective than circular motions that may leave streaks.

A dampened chamois skin held in the other hand can catch any excess water and then be used to dry the glass panes using the same motions as with the washing process. On larger panes, a squeegee may be used to dry off the glass, using the chamois again to catch the water as it is removed and to wipe the sashes dry.

Drinking fountains should be cleaned each week with a soapy sponge. Any discolorations caused by chemicals in the water may require the use of a small amount of non-abrasive cleansing powder. The fountain should then be washed, rinsed, and dried. Water pressure should be checked to insure a stream of water high enough to permit use without the fixture coming into contact with the mouth. If pressure is too strong, water spillage may cause serious damage to walls, floor, and ceilings below.

CLEANING MARBLE

Marble walls, windowsills, and floors should be kept as clean as possible. It is much easier to keep marble clean than to remove stains and dullness after they occur. Paint, varnish, oil, or grease spilled on marble should be wiped off as quickly as possible. Turpentine will aid in removing fresh paint. Soap and water will help remove oil and grease stains. Acid solutions should not be used because they dissolve the marble. If the polished surface of the marble has become dull, it can usually be restored to a glossy appearance by rubbing with putty powder available at most monument works.

CLEANING VARIOUS METALS

Metal surfaces of various kinds will be encountered frequently in the church maintenance program. Hardware on doors and windows, office equipment, storage cabinets, and other metal equipment will require regular maintenance.

The frequency of cleaning will depend upon a variety of factors such as weather, corrosive fumes in the atmosphere, intensity of use, and the level of cleanliness desired.

In cleaning *stainless steel,* soap and water may be used to remove quickly ordinary deposits of dirt and light grease. Stainless steel should be thoroughly rinsed and dried after washing where possible. Other cleaning agents to be used when more thorough cleaning is needed include special stainless steel polishing powder, Bon Ami, or fine pumice. Rubbing should be in the direction of the finish lines. Streaks which may appear after wiping with a damp cloth or sponge can be prevented by adding a small amount of weak citric acid to the dampening solution.

Aluminum is vulnerable to both acids and alkalies. Special mild solvent cleaners of non-etching chemicals should be applied to aluminum surfaces, using 00 steel wool pads for stubborn spots. For routine care, use buffered silicates with silicones as a film former, damp-wiping the aluminum surface. This will remove soil accumulations and oxidation and will form a surface film that gives protection and improves the appearance.

Communionware, offering plates, vases and other items of solid or plated *gold* or *silver* may be washed in hot water and mild soap. Rinse in clean hot water and polish with a soft fine dry cloth. Silver should be polished when discolored with a good quality silver polish. Wash, rinse, and polish with a clean dry cloth. If silver is to be stored, place with flakes or moth crystals in flannel bags. Gold can be cleaned with an ammonia solution. Rinse and polish with clean dry cloths.

Brass, bronze, and *copper* are subject to tarnish and corrosion if not properly cleaned and polished. Commercial polishes are available. An effective cleaner can be made very economically of vinegar and salt. Items washed in this mixture should be rinsed and polished with a clean dry cloth. The green-colored stain caused by oxidation can be removed by using a household ammonia solution. Considerable cleaning time may be saved by covering items of brass, bronze, and copper with a coating of clear lacquer.

Iron and *steel* should be painted immediately upon installation to avoid rust. In preparing for painting or repainting, remove oil, grease, and dirt. Rust may be rubbed off with steel wool and emery paper. The first coat should be of red lead or a similar rust-inhibiting paint.

Pewter may be washed in warm soapy water. Rinse and dry but do not polish. Polishing will remove the soft finish desired in pewter.

Shades, blinds, and drapes should be vacuum cleaned at regular intervals. Similarly, when conditions and appearance require, drapes and shades should be removed and cleaned. If the church has several venetian blinds, it may be well to build a washing and drying rack where the blinds may be taken for thorough cleaning.

CLEANING WALLS AND CEILINGS

Each time a room is cleaned, fingerprints and other soil frequently found around light switches, doors, and stairways should be removed. A spray bottle of synthetic cleaner may be kept on the cleaning cart. This cleaner should be sprayed on a damp sponge and applied directly to the soiled area. Rinsing is unnecessary.

At least monthly, the walls and ceilings should be dusted with a long-handled dust mop.

As local conditions require, walls and ceilings need washing. This may be as often as once a year. In this process, it is important to provide safe scaffolding to make it possible for the worker to reach safely the area to be cleaned. The area should first be dusted to remove cobwebs and loose dust and soil.

In addition to ladders or scaffolds, the worker will need two buckets and two sponges—one of each for the cleaning solution, the other for rinse water. Using a sponge, the cleaning solution should be applied to an area about four by four feet. It is best to wash the ceiling first so that splashing and dripping will not dirty a recently cleaned wall.

If necessary, use a scrub brush to remove any stubborn soil. Then wash out the sponge in the cleaning solution, squeeze dry, and pick up the cleaning solution from the surface. The next step is to take the sponge from the rinse-water bucket and rinse the 4 by 4-foot area just cleaned. Dip it, squeeze it dry and clean, and wipe off the area.

In washing ceilings and walls, use a circular motion on the first application of the cleaning solution with side-to-side and up-and-down motions for removing the cleaning solution and rinsing.

CLEANING REST ROOMS

It is essential for the church to maintain clean, odorless, orderly rest-room areas. These areas of the building should be checked daily whenever the building is open for use. Heavy use may require more frequent checking. Carelessness in cleaning and maintaining these areas can have a very adverse effect on all who use the building.

All rest-room fixtures should be thoroughly cleaned every day that the building is open. A good cleaning compound that combines a detergent, sanitizer, and odor counteractant should be used in cleaning the lavatories, toilets, and urinals. Special care should be given in scrubbing thoroughly with a bowl brush under the rims of toilets and urinals, since these locations are often the sources of offensive odors. Seats should be sponged off with soapy water and dried. Rubber gloves should be kept on the cleaning cart for use when cleaning rest-room fixtures.

Cleaning includes emptying of waste receptacles; servicing soap dispensers, paper-towel dispensers, and toilet-paper holders; dusting windowsills, ledges, partitions; cleaning mirrors, shelves, dispensers, waste receptacles; cleaning partitions, walls, and doors; scrubbing fixtures as previously described and, finally, sweeping and mopping the floor.

Use a damp sponge to wipe clean the towel dispensers, waste receptacles, and any water-splash marks on walls around washbasins and fixtures. Fixtures should be checked to be sure all faucets, drains, and other mechanisms are working properly.

Chapter Summary

1. Most churches need a housecleaning to remove accumulated materials that clutter up the building and constitute a fire hazard.

2. The use of low-maintenance building materials and construction plans can greatly reduce maintenance costs.

3. Cleaning should follow a carefully planned schedule using recommended materials, equipment, and procedures.

Chapter 7

FLOORS

SINCE FLOORS ARE the most used and abused portion of any building, they receive the greatest amount of soil. Cleaning, waxing, and polishing floors is one of the most time-consuming jobs in maintenance work.

Methods and materials used in cleaning any floor will depend on the composition of the floor. A cleaning solution used effectively on one floor area may ruin another type. Record should be kept of the kind of floor covering installed in each area of the building. On a master chart kept in the maintenance headquarters, various types of flooring should be indicated so that the correct type of cleaning materials should be used and others avoided. The chart should indicate the appropriate cleaning materials and procedures for each area.

Cleaning costs of the present flooring should be evaluated. If they seem prohibitive, new floor coverings should be considered. Some types of floor covering may be satisfactory for some areas, yet unsuitable for others. When replacement time comes, try to avoid future maintenance problems by choosing the proper floor-covering materials for each area. Vinyl tile is easier to maintain than rubber tile. It wears better and does not show traffic wear. Marbleized patterns of brown, gray, or green will have lower maintenance costs than those of extremely light colors. Ordinary asphalt tile should not be used in kitchen areas, mechanical rooms, or storage areas where grease, oil, gasoline, or similar materials may be spilled. For such areas a special grease-proof asphalt tile should be secured. For rest rooms, unglazed ceramic tile is preferred. It is hard, smooth, easy to clean, and unaffected by acids and alkalies.

MAINTENANCE PROCEDURES

Specific suggestions for the care of various types of floors will be given later in this chapter. For other than carpet, there are three basic steps in adequate floor care: cleaning, sealing, and maintaining. If floors are not cleaned regularly, dirt imbeds in the floor—whether wood, tile, cork, stone, or carpet. Dirt not only changes the color and general appearance of the floor; it acts as an abrasive and actually cuts the material in the flooring. All dirt and foreign substances should be carefully removed from a floor before new protective materials are applied. If this is not done, the wax or other materials may not perform properly. For example, residue of cleaning materials can seriously hamper the effective application of wax.

Cleaners should be chosen for each type of floor covering. Solvents should never be used on asphalt tile. Oil-emulsion soaps should never be used on rubber flooring materials. Maintenance employees should be careful to follow manufacturers' recommendations regarding the type of cleaner and the concentration recommended for each type of floor.

The second step in floor care is sealing. After careful cleaning, the floor should be sealed with the compound best suited for its type. This will seal off pores, cracks, and crevices that would otherwise collect dirt and absorb grease and grime. Sealing protects and prevents discoloration of the flooring materials.

The third step is the application of wax to provide an attractive surface that will take the brunt of hard wear. If a floor is kept properly waxed, the thin film of wax will protect the underlying floor and will provide a safe, attractive surface.

It is possible to spend large sums on labor, equipment, and materials and still have floors that are unattractive, slippery, or in poor condition. Maintenance personnel must be properly informed and trained in the use of appropriate procedures in caring for each type of floor.

CARPETING

Carpet is frequently installed "wall to wall" in sanctuaries, offices, libraries, conference rooms, parlors, and lounges. Users like its quieting effect and, if properly maintained and cared for, its more attractive appearance. Total costs of installation and maintenance over several years may prove less expensive for carpet than for other floor covering.

Carpets are often used in church buildings because of their acoustical properties which absorb many of the unwanted impact noises that harder surfaces either create or reflect. Women's spike-heeled shoes are usually less destructive to good carpeting than to tile. In using carpeting in the sanctuary, care should be given not to create problems for the musicians by having so much acoustical treatment that the music cannot properly be heard throughout the building.

Weekly vacuum cleaning and annual shampooing usually provide sufficient care for carpets in church buildings. Local factors may require more frequent cleaning. Spots should be removed by detergents or commercial solvents as quickly as possible.

Some object to the use of carpet because of the problem of static electricity, particularly noticeable in northern climates during cold winter months when humidity levels are apt to be low indoors. Some relief is possible by spraying carpeted areas with a water-base solution that adheres to carpet fibers. One spraying provides enough surface moisture to eliminate most static electricity for a period of three to five months.

WOOD FLOORS

No wood floor should be left unprotected. New wood floors or freshly sanded floors are very porous and absorbent. They may deteriorate quickly as a result of the destructive effects of moisture, fungi, or insects if they are not treated properly and promptly.

The National Sanitary Supply Association in a booklet "Modern Floor Care" suggests the following sanding procedures for new floors: "New floors should always be sanded with the grain of the wood. For the first cut, use a medium-grade sandpaper. The second cut can be made with a medium-fine paper, and the third cut with a fine paper. For a smooth finish make a fourth cut with extra-fine paper."

For old floors in bad condition but fairly smooth, they suggest "the first cut should be made with the grain of the wood, using a rough-grade paper. Next, still sanding with the grain, use a medium paper, then a fine paper, and finish with an extra-fine grade of sandpaper."

Old warped or cupped floors in bad condition may require the first cut to be made diagonally across the grain, using a coarse sandpaper. This should be followed by a second cut diagonally opposite to the first. Third, fourth, and fifth sandings would use in turn: rough, medium, and fine grades of sandpaper.

Parquet or patterned-wood floors require special treatment with a disc sander.

"Immediately after sanding, sweep or vacuum the floor thoroughly. Then go over the floor with a 'tack' cloth wrapped around a floor brush. This will pick up any fine dust which may remain even after sweeping. A newly sanded floor should not be washed or wet in any manner. . . . (A tack cloth is a soft cloth which is dampened slightly with mineral spirits or sealer.)" [1]

Before repeated sanding of any floors, consideration should be given to the use of liquid chemical strippers and varnish removers now available. Wood floors should be sanded after removal of the old finish only if the floors are badly scarred, scratched or uneven.

Sealers for Wood Flooring: By applying a sealer to freshly sanded wood floors, one can decrease the absorptive qualities and provide a foundation for a beautiful finish that will require much less maintenance.

There are two basic types of wood sealers—penetrating and surface. Penetrating seals give better protection against moisture and will withstand harder wear.

Applying a sealer requires a much different procedure from that of applying varnish or paint. Employees should note carefully the instructions provided with the sealer by the manufacturer or supplier. Usually two coats of sealer are needed before the floor is ready for waxing. The sealer should be applied immediately after the floors have been sanded or cleaned and dried. Several methods are in common use. Sealer may be brushed on with a wide brush or a clean mop, brushing first across the grain of the wood and then a second time with the grain to spread out any excess. Another method is to apply the seal from a sprinkling can to a section of the floor. After allowing a few minutes for the seal to penetrate, the excess may be removed by pushing it with a floor squeegee over to the next section on the floor. Additional sealer may then be sprinkled on this area as needed, and the process repeated until the entire floor is treated. Any seal not absorbed by the floor

---

[1] *Modern Floor Care,* National Sanitary Supply Association, 159 Dearborn Street, Chicago, Illinois, 1958. Used by permission.

should be rubbed off with clean rags. Buffing the seals after application, with a floor machine equipped with a steel-wool pad, will result in greater penetration of the seal and a harder, longer-wearing finish.

The use of a sealer is recommended because it penetrates further into the wood than paint, varnish, or lacquer. It makes for a denser floor, more capable of withstanding heavy traffic, resisting stains, and moisture. When wax is applied over the sealer and is polished, an extremely hard coating is formed.

RESILIENT FLOOR

Churches are now using large quantities of resilient floor-covering materials. Included in this category are asphalt, vinyl, rubber and cork tile, and linoleum. Some of these materials are quite economical, and all are easily installed and fairly easily maintained with proper equipment. Such floors are called "resilient" or soft because of their capacity to "give" under pressure. Minor scars or indentations tend to disappear because of the elasticity and "cold flow" of the material. Because of their composition, resilient floors absorb some sound—although not as much as carpet.

All resilient floor coverings, including vinyl tile, give better service when protected by a finish coating of wax. Such finishes will minimize scratching, reduce soiling, maintain the gloss, and make regular cleaning easier.

Cleaners or polishes containing any abrasives, oils, or any kind of organic solvents such as gasoline, turpentine, naphtha, or carbon tetrachloride should not be used on asphalt tile. These materials dissolve the asphalt and other materials in the tile and cause serious deterioration.

Cleaning and Treating New Resilient Floors: Clean new resilient floors with a floor brush or vacuum cleaner.

Newly laid tile floors should not be scrubbed until thoroughly set. At least a week is needed to give the adhesive time to set. The floor should not be flooded. Only sufficient water or cleaner to wet the area being worked should be applied. The floor may then be scrubbed with an electric-powered floor machine equipped with a stiff brush to strip the protective film applied at the factory. After scrubbing, the cleaning solution should be removed with a damp mop or with a wet-dry vacuum designed for this purpose. Rinse with clean cold water. Allow floor to dry thoroughly before applying wax finish.

Resilient floors that have been waxed or polished should be cleaned regularly by a floor brush or vacuum cleaner. Clean when necessary with a mop dampened with clean cold water, then buff with a floor machine. Such mopping should not remove the wax. In mopping a waxed floor, effective cleaning may be accomplished by adding a small amount of water-emulsion wax to the mop water instead of a cleaner or a detergent. The wax serves as a detergent in the mopping process and replaces about as much wax as is normally removed in the mopping. One pint of water-emulsion wax of 12 percent solids to three gallons of mop water would be a suitable mixture. If a floor has an adequate coating of wax, simple buffing with a nylon pad on a floor machine will maintain its luster between the more thorough cleaning operations.

Stripping: After continued use, it will be necessary to remove periodically the old floor finish. Once or twice a year should be often enough for this "stripping" of the old finish. Heavy traffic areas may require more frequent care. This can be done by scrubbing, preferably with a powered floor machine using a soft brush. The floor should then be rinsed thoroughly and dried before a new finish is applied. The use of a wet-dry vacuum machine to pick up the scrubbing solution and rinse water will avoid leaving a thin dirty film on the surface and will remove water from joints in the tile where it might damage the adhesive if not removed.

Waxing: Proper waxing is essential to adequate floor care. Many workmen tend to apply a heavy layer of wax, thinking they are thus providing greater protection. When the coating is too heavy, however, the surface of the wax film hardens while the wax underneath does not dry and remains soft. The total wax deposit becomes gummy and traps dirt and grit, thus affording less protection for the floor than would a coat of proper thickness.

For best results, apply three parts of water and one part water-emulsion wax to the clean, dry floor using a clean, fine-strand cloth mop or wool applicator. Dip the mop into the wax mixture, squeeze out the excess and mop the floor from side to side. Before the mop works dry, dip again into the wax, squeeze and apply until the entire floor area is covered except for an area six inches out from the baseboard where there will be no traffic.

Allow to dry for at least fifteen minutes, and buff with a power machine using a soft brush. A second thin coat of wax may then be applied to give a heavier protective coating. Some self-polishing waxes do not require buffing, but if a high polish is desired, buffing will accelerate drying and improve the gloss. Fleeces or carpet pads may be used under a soft brush in buffing.

Where slipperiness is a problem use an anti-slip, water-emulsion finish. Improper waxing procedures may cause slick floors. Reread directions for application of the wax being used. To avoid slickness, allow some waxes to air for several hours before buffing.

Removing Stains from Resilient Flooring:[2] The chart in Figure 5 shows how to remove stains from resilient flooring .

[2] Richard Almy, "Floors Deserve Decent Maintenance," *Protestant Church Buildings and Equipment,* February, 1960, pp. 11f. Used by permission.

Figure 5

Type of Stain	Linoleum, Linotile, Vinyl sheet flooring	Asphalt Tile, Vinyl Asbestos Tile	Rubber Tile, 'Solid' Vinyl Tile, Custom Vinyl, Cork Tile	Cork Tile
Tar, grease, oil, candle wax, chewing gum	3, 8	3, 5, 7, 10	3, 5, 7, 10	3, 8
Rubber—heel marks, shoe polish	8, if stubborn; 5, 10	5, 7, 10	5, 7, 10	8
Coffee, fruit, juice, alcohol, iodine, ink, mercurochrome, mustard, catsup	1, 4, 10 or 5, 7, 10	1, 5, 10, or 5, 7, 10	1, 4, 10 or 5, 7, 10	1, 4, 10 or 5, 9
Cigarette burns, rust, mildew, blood, dye, grass stains	5, 7, 10	5, 7, 10	5, 7, 10	5, 9
Paint, varnish, nail polish, solvents, lacquer, cleaning fluid	1, 4, 10 or 3, 5, 7, 10	1, 4, 10 or 3, 5, 7, 10	1, 4, 10 or 3, 5, 7, 10	1, 4, 10 or 3, 5, 9
Shellac	1, 3, 6, 10 or 6, 10	1, 4, 10 or 6, 10	1, 4, 10 or 6, 10	1, 4, 10 or 6, 10
Acids, lye, alkalies, soap stains	1, 2, 10 or 5, 10	1, 2, 10 or 5, 10	1, 2, 10 or 5, 10	1, 2, 10 or 5, 10

CORK FLOORS

Cork flooring is usually marketed as cork tile. The surface of the tile has been treated with a coat of wax or with a coat of wax and resin. Cork tile is relatively soft and can be damaged by sharp impacts or by small furniture rests. Cork is also easily damaged by grit and soil and therefore requires more frequent cleaning than other floor coverings. Only mild or neutral cleaners should be used with cork. High-alkaline cleaners deteriorate the cork, making it brittle, and will sometimes cause whitening. Note preceding chart for recommended stain-removal procedures.

CONCRETE FLOORS

Concrete is a mixture of portland cement, sand, gravel, and water. The lime in the cement is alkaline, and therefore only those flooring materials or paints that are resistant to alkaline action should be used on concrete floors. Paint for concrete floors should be chosen carefully to be sure it is suitable and that it is applied according to the manufacturer's instructions.

Unpainted or uncovered floors will be more easily cleaned and will give better service if properly sealed.

Figure 5. 1. If freshly spilled, take up immediately with blotting action. 2. Wash area with rag dipped in water. 3. If dry, remove excess with putty knife. 4. Wash with cloth dipped in a chemically neutral liquid cleaner, then rinse. 5. Rub with #0 steel wool in a chemically neutral cleaner, then rinse. 6. Rub lightly with cloth dipped in alcohol, then rinse. 7. If method 5 fails, dust with mild household abrasive cleaner, then rub with #0 steel wool dipped in a chemically neutral liquid cleaner. Rinse. 8. Rub lightly with cloth or #0 steel wool to which a solvent wax has been applied. Wipe with clean cloth before wax dries completely. Buff when dry. 9. Sand deep stains with #00 sandpaper, then apply paste wax. Buff. 10. Wax when the area is dry.

Sealing provides a hard, smooth surface that can be mopped easily and quickly and will not trap dust and soil. The first step is to clean the floor by thorough scrubbing with a hot neutral cleaning solution. Wetting down the floor before washing it will improve results. After scrubbing, the floor should be rinsed with clear water.

Before sealing, the floor should be etched with a solution of one part muriatic acid to four parts of water. This solution should remain on the floor for fifteen to thirty minutes, then should be flushed off with clean water and rinsed a second time. After the floor has dried thoroughly, apply a concrete sealer according to the manufacturer's directions.

Unless properly sealed, a dry cement floor will absorb alkaline salts that will crystallize in the pores of the cement. Moisture will then enlarge the pores and eventually cause a surface powdering called dusting or blooming.

CERAMIC-TILE FLOORS

Ceramic-tile floors are extremely durable, easily cleaned, and quite attractive for certain areas. The main precaution is to avoid the use of strong alkaline solutions that may disintegrate the grout around the tile. A penetrating finish seal may be used to protect the tile, and especially the grout, from water penetration, stains, and the wear of heavy traffic. If a high-gloss appearance is desired, ceramic tile may be waxed, preferably with a non-slip, water-emulsion wax. Varnish or lacquer should never be used on ceramic tile.

Routine cleaning involves sweeping or vacuuming after use. Use a damp mop to remove dirt. A liquid synthetic detergent in hot water makes a satisfactory cleaner. After the floor is thoroughly clean and dry, it may be buffed or, if desired, a wax finish may be applied over the seal.

Because of their inherent slip hazard, tile floors should be kept dry at all times.

Quarry tile provides a very durable and easily cleaned floor. It is particularly suitable in kitchens and other areas where moisture is a problem.

TERRAZZO FLOORS

Terrazzo floors are made of 70 percent or more of marble chips set in a matrix of 30 percent or less of portland cement. Properly maintained, they present a gleaming, attractive appearance for many years of hard usage.

Terrazzo floors should be sealed to close the pores in the marble and in the matrix and prevent their enlargement. Sealer also makes the floor easier to clean. Two thin coats of sealer are better than a single heavy coat. Apply first to base, corners, and edges and then to floor surface, wiping it on with an applicator or cloth. Allow one day for drying before applying second coat. If a glossier appearance is desired, a thin coat of water-emulsion wax or slip-proof polymeric finish may be applied. Damp mopping and machine buffing will restore the finished appearance. Sealer should be applied only after thorough cleaning. After sealing, allow at least six hours before using the floor and twenty-four hours before waxing.

Do not use any kind of acids, alkaline salt cleaners, steel wool, or harsh abrasives on terrazzo. Acids will dissolve the marble chips, some alkaline salts will cause disintegration, steel-wool particles may remain to rust and stain the floor. Avoid using oily dust mops or sweeping compounds on terrazzo. Use only *wax-based* mop treatments or sweeping compounds, if used at all.

MARBLE FLOORS

Routine maintenance is relatively simple and easy. Sweeping and vacuuming, with damp mopping when needed, is usually sufficient. When cleaning marble, use only neutral cleaning solutions. The warnings previously given about the use of acids, alkalies, and oils on terazzo apply also to marble. When marble floors are in extremely soiled condition, a powdered cleaner may be used. The floor should be wet with clear water. The powder may then be sprinkled on the surface and allowed to remain until dissolved. Scrub with a brush or a floor machine equipped with a bassine fiber brush. Sprinkle additional powder on any stubborn spots until they are removed. Wash off the cleaning solution, then rinse. Remove all water spots to avoid streaking. After floors have dried, a sealer and then wax may be applied. These are usually not needed on marble unless the floor has gotten in poor condition.

Chapter Summary

1. Floor care is one of the most important and most expensive aspects of property maintenance.

2. Best results require powered floor machines and materials suited to the type of floor in each area.

3. Carpets absorb many impact noises and are thought to be less expensive to maintain than many other types of floor covering.

4. Noncarpeted areas should be cleaned, sealed, and waxed on a regular schedule.

Chapter 8

PAINTS AND ACOUSTICS

A MAJOR ITEM in any maintenance program is that of painting and redecorating both the interior and exterior of the building. The condition of painted surfaces is a major factor in the church's public relations.

The primary purpose of exterior painting is the protection of exposed surfaces. A secondary purpose is the improvement of appearance.

Interior painting is primarily for decoration and light reflection and only incidentally for protection and preservation of exposed surfaces. Proper interior painting and subsequent cleaning provide an atmosphere of cleanliness, orderliness, and beauty.

Churches have often been unduly unimaginative in their choice of paint colors. Colors have a definite psychological influence on moods and emotions. Choosing the proper colors can help create the desired climate for learning, worship, or activity. When people buy new clothes, they usually like to get a suit or a dress of a different color from one they already have. This is a good principle to follow in painting a church building. Use paint to decorate, to give a lift, to set a tone, to create a mood—not just to cover up a dirty wall. Decide what effect you need to create in each area and then consult the representative of a paint company for expert advice as to the proper paints and colors to achieve the desired results.

Man should use all his senses in his worship of God. There is a ministry of color just as there is a ministry of words and music. Beautiful color, called by some "silent music," can be one of many pathways to God. Since color can contribute so much to worship and to learning, the fullest and best use should be made of it. It is usually no more expensive to choose a good color than a poor one.

RECORD KEEPING

Records should be kept on major interior and exterior paint jobs. List each room by number of location and record in detail information about all painting, plastering, washing, or other treatment. Date, type of paint or other material used, source of supply, and the individual or company doing the work, should be recorded in the church maintenance files.

Each coat of paint becomes the undercoat for all future applications, unless expensive removal is to be involved. Great care should, therefore, be taken in choosing exactly the right type of paint and in applying it so that it is securely anchored to the surface or to the previous coat of paint.

Some materials in previously used paint may be incompatible with newly applied paint, resulting in an unsatisfactory appearance. Accurate information about previous painting can help in making the right choice of material.

EXTERIOR PAINTING

The need for repainting exterior surfaces will vary according to climatic conditions and such other factors as exposure to sun, smoke, fumes, and dust. Normally, outside painting should be done every three to five years. Steel sash should be painted every fifth year, wood sash every fourth year, and masonry surfaces every seven or eight years. The bottom rails of sashes and sills, and frames of either wood or metal should be repainted every two or three years.

In cold climates, alternate thawing and freezing may break open the paint surface, allowing water to penetrate to the wood or metal underneath. This will cause rot or rust if not corrected by repainting.

Responsible church officials, familiar with local conditions, will know how to schedule painting to provide "preventive maintenance." It is much easier and much less expensive in the long run to keep exterior surfaces properly painted than it is to scrape, brush, or burn off cracked, peeled, or blistered paint that has deteriorated and allowed exposed surfaces to deteriorate.

In the initial maintenance survey and in each subsequent inspection, the condition of exterior surfaces should be examined and areas needing paint should be given immediate attention.

Considerable money can often be saved by consulting a competent paint specialist available through paint manufacturers or distributors. He should be able to recommend the proper type of paint to use on each surface to be painted, both inside and out. A record of such recommendations should be filed in the maintenance office with the record of all painting and decorating done.

Buying cheap paint is usually false economy. It usually costs about three or four times as much to apply the paint as it does to buy it. Using the best materials and workmanship will help make the building attractive for a 4- or 5-year period. Cheap paints inexpertly applied may not last more than two years. Before deciding to save money on using cheaper materials, figure out the cost per year for painting when labor and other expenses have been added to the cost of the paint.

INTERIOR PAINTING

Interior painting involves primarily walls, ceilings, doors, windows, some furniture, and play equipment. How frequently this painting needs to be done depends on the amount and kind of use and the possibility of washing rather than repainting the painted areas. Several public school systems have found that washing ceilings and walls, using appropriate cleaning solutions and proper equipment, can reduce considerably the need for repainting—and consequently the total cost of maintenance. A thorough washing will probably cost about one-fourth as much as a new paint job.

In painting the interior of the sanctuary, colors that are conducive to worship should be chosen. The Department of Church Building of the National Council of Churches says churches would benefit from more light and a better use of color. Our new churches need to give these matters careful thought.

"Light and color cannot be separated, for color is nothing but fragmented light. In actual practice, the color of a wall depends fully as much upon the character and intensity of the light which falls upon it as upon the pigments which have been spread over the surface." Consequently, they recommend that "the only place to choose the colors for a church is in the room where they are to be used. . . . Rarely is the light in a church pure daylight; often it is filtered through colored glass, or even the foliage of surrounding trees, with the result that it is refracted. Colors for a church should be selected in full daylight and then tested both at dusk and by artificial light. This is particularly necessary with greens." [1]

[1] *Light and Color,* published by The Department of Church Building, National Council of Churches, 475 Riverside Drive, New York, N.Y., pp. 1-5, copyright 1956. Used with permission.

In choosing paint colors for rooms used for education and for offices, it is well to remember that "light colors seem to move away from us; dark colors seem to come near to us. To 'push out' any surface, we make it lighter than the areas around it; to draw a wall toward us, we darken it. Light colors give perspective and dignity; dark colors are more intimate and informal.

"To be livable, a room must have color balance. This can be achieved either by compromise or by contrast. The neutral colors, such as gray and tan, are soothing. Our fathers used them to produce peaceful churches in which sleep was not difficult. The more contrast there is in a church the more exciting it becomes, and the more skill is needed in getting the colors just right."[2]

Considerable economy can be achieved by adopting a uniform standard of materials to be used in all areas of the building. Several colors of paint of the best quality from a single manufacturer can be chosen so that all classrooms in a given area need not be painted the same color. These same colors, however, may be used in other sections of the building. By using varied colors of the same kind of paint throughout the interior, one can provide variety yet avoid the problems of incompatibility often encountered when different paints of differing chemical composition are used in successive applications.

Most paint manufacturers provide to churches free consultation service regarding types of paint and colors. Churches should obtain such advice before adopting a long-range painting schedule, a painting color scheme, or policies regarding the application of paint by volunteer

[2] *Ibid.* pp. 3-4. See also Henry L. Wright and Foster K. Sampson in "Design," in *The Nation's Schools,* Volume 66, Number 3, September 1960, for directions for selecting appropriate colors for ceilings and walls of education buildings. Wright and Sampson recommend that paint used in education areas have a reflectance factor of 80 percent or more for ceilings, 60 percent or more for walls.

workers. Architects can supply information and recommendations regarding color schemes and the most satisfactory materials for use in various sections of buildings.

JOB CONTRACT CONSIDERATIONS

Some churches will find it more satisfactory to contract some or all of their painting work than to have it done by their maintenance staff or by volunteers. Rooms with high ceilings, where extensive equipment is needed to reach the surfaces to be painted, should usually be painted by contract for reasons of economy and safety.

In securing bids and in letting contracts it is important to know and to incorporate certain vital information into the contracts and bids. Contracts should be in writing and should include specific information regarding the cost, terms of payment, dates for beginning and completing the work, and the scope of the work that would involve the furnishing of all labor, tools, ladders, other equipment, paint, and other materials needed to complete the painting and to restore the building to use. The contract should indicate the rooms or other areas to be painted, the kind and extent of surface preparation to be done by the painters, the kind of paint to be applied, colors, number of coats, workmanship, protection of furnishings and floors, and removal of all tools, materials, scaffolds and waste so as to return the building to usable condition.

C. A. March suggests the following sample specifications for a painting contract:[3]

Instructions to Bidders. The conditions and instructions to bidders, as applied on the general contract, apply also on the painting contract.

Scope of Work. The work to be done by the painting con-

[3] C. A. March, *Building Operation and Maintenance* (New York: McGraw-Hill Book Company, Inc., 1950), pp. 241-243. Used by permission of the author.

tractor includes the furnishing of all material, labor, tools, and equipment which shall be required to complete the painting and finishing of the buildings as specified.

Workmanship. All work shall be done in a workmanlike manner by skilled mechanics. All materials shall be evenly spread and smoothly flowed on and shall be free from runs or sags; and no paint, varnish, or enamel shall be applied until preceding coat is thoroughly dry and hard.

No exterior painting shall be done in rainy, damp, or frosty weather, or until surface is thoroughly dry.

No interior painting or finishing shall be permitted until building has been thoroughly dried out.

In general and unless otherwise recommended and specified, exterior oil paints shall be allowed to dry at least 48 hr. between coats, and interior paints shall be allowed to dry at least 24 hr. between coats.

Enamels and varnishes shall be allowed to dry at least 48 hr. between coats, unless noted in the detail specifications, and shall be sanded lightly between coats with No. 0 sandpaper and dusted before succeeding coat is applied.

After paste wood fillers are applied, excess shall be carefully and neatly cleaned from surface by rubbing across grain. All nail holes shall be filled with putty, tinted to match finish.

Preparation of Surfaces. Painting contractor shall be wholly responsible for finish of his work and therefore shall not commence any part of it until surface is in proper condition in every respect. If painting contractor considers any surface so unsuitable for proper finish of his work that it cannot be rectified by slight sanding, he shall note this fact in writing before any materials are applied, and he shall not apply any material until the unsuitable surfaces have been made satisfactory.

All knots or sappy spots shall be given one coat of shellac at least 10 hr. before painting.

All necessary puttying of nail holes, cracks, and blemishes shall be done after priming coat has become hard and dry and before second coat is applied, and putty shall match the shade of finish coat.

On old paint the surfaces shall be first brushed with a wire brush or sanded, and where it is scaling badly, shall be scraped or burned off.

All greasy or oily metal surfaces shall be cleaned with turpentine or naphtha before applying any materials. All scale or rust shall be removed by scraping, wire-brushing, or sandblasting.

Materials. All materials used under painting contract shall be as specified and shall be delivered on the work in the original sealed containers.

All mixing required shall be done on premises, and materials shall be thoroughly stirred and agitated. No materials shall be reduced or changed in any way except as and when specified, and thinners must be pure.

Protection of Property. Painting contractor shall be responsible for condition of building in his charge. He shall protect adjacent work and materials as well as his own.

Inspection. Every facility shall be provided for inspection of work at any time by manager or his authorized representative. Any work not conforming to these specifications shall be cleaned off and repainted at expense of painting contractor.

Removal. When work is completed, the painting contractor shall remove all surplus materials, scaffolds, etc., and he shall clean off all misplaced paint, varnish, or enamel, so as to leave premises in perfect condition.

In actually awarding a contract to a particularly low bidder, it is wise to consider his reputation carefully. It is well to be skeptical of any bid that is too far out of line. Material and labor costs, in theory at least, are substantially the same for competing contractors. Consequently, any difference in price must be accounted for by one or more of these factors: (1) a lower profit expectation, (2) better management of men, material, and equipment, (3) lower overhead, or (4) reliance on cheating on the job.

The burden of proof of intent should be placed on an extremely low bidder before the job is awarded to him.

PAINTING BY VOLUNTEER LABOR

Much of the cost of redecorating is in the labor. Consequently, many church members have made substantial contributions by giving their labor. Contrary to some commonly held conceptions, painting done properly requires considerable skill and knowledge of materials and equipment. Consequently, an experienced painter should supervise all volunteer workers to ensure that proper materials are obtained, that adequate surface preparation is made, and that the materials are applied in the proper manner. With the improvements that have been made in paints in recent years, it is possible to have very excellent results if the proper choice of paint for the surface is made and if the surface has been properly prepared and paint properly applied.

PREPARATORY MEASURES

The best of paints and skilled application cannot produce a satisfactory job unless the surface to be painted is properly prepared. The surface should be clean, smooth, and dry. When heavily varnished wood panels are being painted over in light color, several steps may be necessary to ensure an attractive and lasting job. To prevent old varnish or paint from "bleeding through" it may be necessary to apply a first coat of stain sealer or of aluminum paint.

In painting new plaster less than a year old the presence of free lime in the plaster may react to oils in the paint. To neutralize this action, the plaster wall may be brushed with a solution made by mixing one pound of zinc sulfate in a gallon of water. After allowing the plaster to dry for three days, any crystals that have formed on the surface should be brushed off before the first coat of paint is applied. Be sure to follow instructions of the paint manufacturer in choosing the material for the first or "sizing" coat. No sizing coat is ordinarily needed in painting plasterboard or wallboard except when oil paints are used.

When painting over wood, all knots and sappy spots should be spot painted with shellac to prevent sap or resin "bleeding" through.

If old paint has become cracked, peeled, or brittle, it is advisable to remove it, if an attractive new finish is desired. This can be done by brushing off with an electric-powered brush, a hand brush, or removal by blowtorch. Portable propane-fueled burning torches are recommended but should not be used by amateurs unless precautions are taken against the risk of fire. Chemical paint removers such as caustic soda solutions are not recommended. It is difficult to wash off the solution completely and the action of the solution in raising the grain in the wood leaves an unattractive surface for painting. Nail holes and cracks should be filled with putty before applying the final coat of paint.

In painting old plaster all cracks and holes should be filled. Loose plaster should be removed and the cracks should be dug out so that they are wider near the lath than on the surface. Then when spackling compound or patching plaster is pressed into the cracks, it will lock the patch in place as it dries. After they have dried thoroughly, patches should be sanded down level with the other surface.

Galvanized-metal surfaces present difficulties unless proper preparation is made for painting. They should be washed with a solution made by dissolving one pound of copper sulfate crystals in a gallon of water. Applied with a sponge or brush, this should remain until the surface turns black, indicating that the desired chemical reaction has occurred. The surface should then be rinsed thoroughly with water. The first coat should be a metal primer produced for this particular type of surface.

Whenever painting over glossy painted or enameled surfaces, the gloss should be removed by light sanding, brushing with a special compound, or washing with a strong cleaning powder. If this is not done, the new coat of paint may not adhere to the surface and thus may peel off or break loose under any kind of blow.

Greasy, dusty, or grimy walls should be cleaned before painting. Brushing or vacuuming will remove loose soil, but washing may be necessary to remove grease and grime.

WATERPROOFING LEAKY WALLS

Before applying paint to a wall where previous coats of paint are peeling, careful investigation should be made to determine whether moisture, the most frequent cause of peeling paint, is present. Water penetration should be eliminated before new paint is applied.

Common causes of water penetration beneath paint surfaces include leaking roofs, gutters, and downspouts. Loose mortar joints or "separation cracks" in brick and stone buildings also allow water to seep through, as do bricks and stones themselves if they are very porous. Where construction procedures have not provided a dead-air space, this seepage through the masonry may reach inside walls. Most water problems are caused by improper construction methods or poor materials. Yet many difficult problems of water penetration can be solved.

In masonry walls, it may be necessary to rake out the old mortar joints and refill with nonshrinking mortar. This is an expensive process and will not always completely solve the problems of water penetration if cracked or otherwise imperfect brick or stone remain in the wall. Some painting contractors recommend replacement of all broken or imperfect brick or stone, raking out of mortar joints, and caulking with a polysulfide sealant. The wall is then dampened, and a special grout is applied, using a stiff brush and sponge with a circular motion to ensure that all cracks, joints, and crevices are filled. Brick surfaces should then be wiped, leaving surfaces clean and all cracks filled. With this kind of exterior treatment, the interior walls can be cleaned, smoothed, prepared, and painted.

The property management committee, in making an inspection of the entire building at least annually, should check carefully for possible sources of water damage. Water from leaking roofs or walls will quickly disintegrate plaster, cause paint to peel, rot timber, rust metal, and short out electrical wiring. Sources of water should be stopped before painting. Paint will soon peel from a surface that is exposed to moisture.

PAINTING CONCRETE FLOORS

Synthetic rubber-base sealers and paints are recommended for concrete floors, since they are not adversely affected by moisture and alkali from the concrete. A clear, nonpigmented rubber-base sealer is applied first, then the colored sealer or paint. After the paint has dried thoroughly, a wax coating should be applied to protect the paint or sealer and to make regular cleaning much easier.

SOLVING ACOUSTICAL PROBLEMS

The use of contemporary building materials such as concrete, steel, tile, marble, and plaster, although structurally and economically attractive, often creates acoustical problems. Fortunately, considerable progress has been made in recent years in understanding what causes poor acoustics in a building and in discovering effective means of remedying the problems. Good auditory conditions are no longer a matter of chance. The pastor, organist, and choir need no longer struggle to be heard, nor do the members of the congregation need to endure the reverberating echoes, the garbled words and music, and the distracting noises that often in the past hindered worship or learning.

Such encouraging developments are the result of careful research. To secure good results in any given building will require a carefully calculated balance between sound-conditioning materials, the design of the various rooms, and the materials used in construction. Too extensive use of acoustical plaster or tiles, carpets, cushioned pews, and drapes can result in a "dead" room that will frustrate the musicians and disappoint the worshippers. The ideal is to attain optimum hearing conditions and control of background or extraneous noises. It is not desirable to "soundproof" a room. A certain amount of reverberation is desirable to keep the room "alive," to provide resonance.

In a sanctuary or auditorium, it is desirable that the sound of the voices of the pastor and choir be transmitted to the congregation and that the voices of the congregation be heard in song, scripture reading, and prayer. But some sounds are unwelcome. These include traffic noises outside, foot traffic and conversations in the hallways, and noise from equipment such as organ blowers and heating and ventilating equipment. Sounds that are desirable in one room may be obnoxious to those in adjoining rooms. Acoustical problems are twofold: (1) control of sound originating within a room, and (2) protection of a room from outside sounds.

In essence, sound is composed of waves of air spreading out in all directions from the source. On reaching a wall, floor or ceiling of a room, or an object within the room, the sound waves are reflected and/or absorbed, depending upon the composition of the surface they strike. A soft, porous surface, such as a floor carpet, may absorb nearly all the sound waves. A hard-surfaced plastered wall or a stone floor will absorb very little but will "bounce off" the sound waves in other directions, causing reverberations or echoes as they continue to bounce off other surfaces. This process of multiple reflection prolongs the original sound and causes it to overlap with successive words from the speaker or notes from the musicians, making it difficult to hear or understand.

The ability of a structure or a given surface to resist or reflect sound is determined by its density and resistance to air flow. Heavy, solid walls will stop most noise but the use of lighter-weight construction often does not provide the sound inhibitors needed. Wherever air can pass, either directly or indirectly, through a given material or space, sound-leakage problems occur. Airborne sound is easier to control than percussion sounds. Spike heels on a floor above may sound like a pile driver in an untreated room underneath.

Sound absorption by acoustical materials is determined by the amount of reflected sound that can be absorbed by a given area of that material. Acoustical tiles and other acoustical treatments can now absorb from 70 to 85 percent of reflected noise. They break up the echoing chain of reverberation.

It is neither necessary nor economical to add further acoustical treatment after the desired result has been attained. Too much acoustical treatment makes a room unsuitable for music that needs longer reverberation time. Too little makes it difficult to understand clearly spoken words. Filling a church with people is a much better acoustical treatment than is the lining of its walls and ceilings with sound-absorbing materials.

Around noisy machinery or other sound-producing places such as music studios and rehearsal areas, it may be necessary to use more acoustical materials with a higher noise-reduction effect. Particular care should be exercised in remodeling or in installing heating or air-conditioning equipment to prevent ducts and pipes from becoming troublesome sound-transmitters.

MAINTAINING ACOUSTICAL MATERIALS

Acoustical plaster usually is very soft and very easily dented and scraped. In areas where it has been used, great care should be taken to avoid scraping the ceiling with ladders and other objects. Methods of cleaning acoustical tiles on ceilings and walls are determined by the type of tile, its finish, and the type of soil to be removed. Some tiles are washable and can be cleaned with a damp sponge and soap or detergent. Loose dirt can be removed by brushing or vacuuming, preferably the latter because it prevents rubbing soil into the surface. Nonwashable tiles usually can be cleaned with wallpaper cleaner. An art gum eraser may be used on stubborn marks and smudges.

Chapter Summary

1. Painting protects exposed surfaces and improves appearance. Surfaces should be properly prepared before paint is applied.

2. Records should be kept on major paint jobs, indicating the date last painted, type of paint used, by whom applied, cost, and the recommended date for next painting.

3. Sound may be controlled by the installation of acoustical materials.

Chapter 9

UTILITIES SYSTEMS

MODERN CHURCHES have quite complicated systems of sound amplification, lighting, plumbing, heating, cooling, and other utilities. The maintenance staff should know how to operate these systems and should be able to make at least minor repairs in the event of an emergency.

SOUND-AMPLIFICATION SYSTEMS

Included in this category are intercommunication and public-address equipment, bells, fire alarms, sound motion-picture projectors, tape recorders, and record players. If public-address equipment is not used regularly, the amplifiers should be turned on for half an hour once a week to prevent damage from moisture. When not in use, such equipment should be stored in a dry location.

LIGHTING SYSTEMS

Illumination serves a variety of uses. A well-planned lighting system provides not only adequate visibility but also proper atmosphere and appearance. Beauty, durability, and ease of maintenance should be considered in choosing lighting fixtures. Careful choice and proper installation can reduce considerably the cost of cleaning and relamping. The more accessible the fixture, the less dirt it collects, the easier it is to clean, the lower the maintenance costs. The design of the fixture and the kind of materials used greatly influence the amount of cleaning needed.

Some fixtures are very expensive to maintain because of the difficulty of replacing bulbs. For example, some luminous ceilings require removal of a large section of the ceiling to replace a single lamp. Some plastic materials may become brittle, discolored, or misshapen with continued use. Others may develop static electricity, which attracts dust. Fixtures having grilles for covers are quite hard to clean. Smooth glass is much easier to maintain than are most other materials.

Incandescent or Fluorescent? The choice of type of light should depend on the uses to be made of the area and the desired atmosphere and appearance. Purchase and installation costs of incandescent lighting usually are lower, but operating costs are higher. Fluorescent systems cost more, but they produce much more light per watt of electricity used.

AMOUNT OF LIGHT NEEDED

The quantity of light in any area is measured in footcandles. Lightmeters, available at all electric-supply stores, are used to determine the amount of light provided. The following are minimum levels of lighting for various areas of space in church buildings:

Areas of Space in Building	Minimum Footcandles Needed
Auditoriums	10
Dining Rooms	10
Kitchens	20
Classrooms	30
Offices	50

The amount of lighting needed depends to a great extent on the color of the ceilings, walls, floors, pews, chairs, tables, and other equipment that may either reflect or absorb light. Accumulated dirt on lamp fixtures, walls, and ceilings can waste half of the electric power used for lighting. The cost of cleaning is usually less than the cost of the extra electric power needed to get adequate light through dirty fixtures.

MAINTENANCE

Proper maintenance can reduce costs and improve appearance. Most fixtures need cleaning at least monthly. The technique of cleaning depends on the type of fixture. Wipe off loose dirt with a treated dustcloth. Remove grease film or other soil with a sponge. Examine for defective bulbs, sockets, or wiring. As a safety precaution, electricity should be turned off before cleaning a light fixture to facilitate cleaning and making minor repairs and to avoid danger of an electric shock. Use of a sturdy stepladder provides not only a place for a pail of cleaning solution, but also a safe access to the fixture.

HEATING AND COOLING SYSTEMS

Programs of many churches are seriously and needlessly hampered by inadequate heating systems. In some cases, only portions of the building can be heated satisfactorily. This places restrictions on full use of the building. Churches should have a policy designed to ensure that the program, not the building, be given priority. If improved maintenance procedures, and even some major overhauling of the heating system, are necessary to make the building available for full use, then these courses should be followed.

A basic problem in maintaining heat is that of reducing the amount of exposure to cold weather. A careful examination of the building should reveal any major sources of cold air and avenues of escape of warm air. Trouble spots include cracked windows, ill-fitting doors and windows, and poorly constructed floors and walls. Excessive opening and closing of doors, of course, wastes considerable heat. Warm air within the building may also escape through ceilings and walls. Hot air naturally moves up, not sideways or down. Consequently, a well-insulated ceiling overhead prevents warm air from escaping and thus from pulling in cold air drafts as it moves up and out. A snow-free roof immediately after a light snow is proof of where much of the heat is going. Heat coming through the ceiling and roof of an uninsulated building soon melts off the snow. By cutting off this flow of air, considerable heat loss is stopped, usually enough in two or three years to justify the cost of insulation.

Some churches are now using radiant heating, which depends upon convection rather than air currents. Although heating elements may be imbedded in the floor, ceiling, or walls, they are usually installed in a concrete floor. Radiant heat provides heat where it is needed for the comfort of all.

Heat can be also supplied by various kinds of perimeter-heating plans, which use baseboard convectors along the entire wall rather than radiators or a single outlet for forced air. Because of the frequent combination of heating and cooling, more and more churches are using systems that do both jobs. This can be achieved by supplying central forced air (either chilled or heated) or by utilizing convectors with chilled, warm, or hot water. Larger churches should seriously consider the wisdom of providing a zoning arrangement that heats or air-conditions only the parts of the building that need to be heated or cooled to the comfort level. Such zoning permits heating and cooling of other areas of the building to be maintained at minimum levels, yet be quickly and safely brought to comfortable levels when needed.

Heating costs can be reduced considerably by insulating floors, ceilings, and walls. Weatherstripping of windows and doors and installation of storm windows and doors further reduce exposure to cold weather and thus lower heating costs. Doors and windows should be caulked to reduce flow of cold air through cracks around window and door frames.

Routine Care: Most heating and cooling systems are complicated and expensive. Probably the most important thing to remember about them is that they function more satisfactorily and last longer with regular lubrication. Routine steps that should be taken to keep heating and air-conditioning systems in good operating condition are described in the instruction and maintenance manuals supplied by manufacturers and distributors of the particular equipment. By referring to these manuals, the maintenance staff can phase into their scheduled activities the necessary care and upkeep of this equipment.

Compressors, pumps, fans, motors, and other equipment with moving parts should be inspected weekly, and any corrective maintenance that may be needed should be taken care of immediately. The manufacturer's recommendations should be followed in the choice and use of lubricants and in other servicing. Use of a checklist for marking dates of inspection and for recording service performed can help make certain that no equipment is neglected.

Controls: Control mechanisms of heating and cooling systems are quite intricate and should be serviced only by those qualified by training and experience. Churches should usually contract with a dependable service agency to inspect, adjust, and repair control mechanisms periodically and as needed.

Forced-air heating and cooling systems require that filters be cleaned and replaced regularly. Dirty filters and ducts can waste considerable heat and power. At the beginning and end of each heating season, and of each cooling season, the pipes and valves should be thoroughly checked for leaks, corrosion, faulty insulation, and other defects. Off-season corrective and preventive maintenance is less expensive and much more convenient than emergency measures performed in midseason.

PLUMBING SYSTEMS

Property maintenance includes regular inspection and upkeep of plumbing facilities. Plumbing skills are essential in the installation and maintenance of water supply lines, drainage lines, and heating and cooling equipment. Plumbing fixtures in rest rooms serving preschool children should be at the proper height. Water-closet bowls for this age group should be ten inches high, and lavatories sixteen to eighteen inches high. For primary and junior children, water-closet bowls should be thirteen inches high. Wall-hung urinals for boys should be no more than eighteen inches high. Wall-hung fixtures for rest rooms make possible faster and better cleaning. Toilet water-closet bowls should be of the elongated type with open-front plastic seats.

Drinking fountains of the wall-hung type are easier to clean than are other types. If located in hallways, they should be recessed and away from stairs so as not to impede traffic. An additional fitting can be installed at a lower level on most coolers to accommodate smaller children. This obviates the building of steps that interfere with safe traffic and easy cleaning.

Consistent use of fixtures and faucets from the same manufacturer facilitates procurement of replacement parts when needed. Plumbing repairs can be speeded up by identifying various pipelines with a distinctive color. For instance, hot water lines may be marked by a red tag or by red paint on valves or connections. Cold water lines may be marked blue, gas lines green, waste lines yellow, and vent pipes black. Hot water lines and steam

pipes should be insulated. Cold water lines that cause
condensation and dripping should also be covered.

Maintenance personnel should master the use of the
"plumbers friend" and the wire and rod devices designed
to clear out clogged water closets and drainage lines.
They should be able also to change faucet washers and
to service toilet fixtures. People using church facilities
almost invariably expect the plumbing system to be clean
and in good working order.

Chapter Summary

1. Adequate utilities systems enable a church to accomplish more effectively its objective of reaching and serving
more people.

2. Proper cleaning of light fixtures, ceilings, and walls can
improve lighting and reduce power costs.

3. Proper insulation of building, pipes, and ducts can
reduce heating costs.

4. Heating and cooling systems demand consistent care
and operation for trouble-free service.

5. Provision of a zoning arrangement that heats or air-
conditions only the sections of the building being used
should be seriously considered by large churches.

Chapter 10

FURNITURE
AND EQUIPMENT

FOR EACH ITEM of its furniture and equipment, the church should have at least one copy of any available instructions that may be needed for operation and maintenance. Also, the church office should keep inventory and service records of all furniture and equipment.

PIANOS

Piano maintenance problems can be kept to a minimum through a wise choice of instruments at the time of purchase. The useful life of a piano depends largely on the quality of its materials and craftsmanship and the kind of care it receives. A new piano should be tuned three or four times during the first year. Piano dealers usually provide a tuning and a regulation of the action at the time the new instrument is delivered and, sometimes, a second or third tuning later in the first year of service. Thereafter, the church should provide for regular tuning and repair.

Purchase of a good, used grand piano for the church auditorium may be more prudent than purchasing a new spinet. The longer strings of the grand give greater resonance and more sonorous tone quality. Purchase of a low-priced spinet piano may prove disappointing because of the more limited time of satisfactory service that may be expected. Some manufacturers build special-model spinets for churches and schools. These sturdy, well-built instruments often prove quite satisfactory for education assembly areas and classrooms.

Routine Care: A piano cannot give effective service or remain in attractive condition unless it is properly maintained. Although the piano mechanism is quite delicate, it is astonishingly durable when given proper care. Aspects of piano maintenance that should be provided by the custodial staff include regular cleaning, polishing, and waxing. Inasmuch as extreme changes of temperature and humidity are hard on pianos, they should not be placed close to radiators or heating outlets.

The lid covering the piano keyboard should be kept closed when the instrument is being cleaned and dusted. Furniture polish or oil on the tuning pins causes the piano to get out of tune. The piano should be kept clear of hymnbooks, literature, flowers, and ornaments.

Dust the piano with a soft, clean cloth. Clean the keys with a slightly dampened sponge. Never use soapy water. Rub the keys the length of the key rather than sideways across the keys. This prevents dampness getting between or below the keys, endangering the action.

Service Contracts: Most churches will find that an annual service contract covering the tuning and repairing of all church pianos and organs will not only give better service from the instruments but will save money in the long run. Repairs are much less expensive if made when difficulties begin to appear. The company offering the service contract should have available technicians who are able to tune and to make minor repairs to the pianos, such as the replacement of tuning pins, keyboard ivory, felts, hammers, and other minor parts. The contract should indicate the number of times per year the instrument will be tuned, the nature of repairs that will be made without extra charge, the availability of emergency service if needed. When major repairs not covered by the service contract are needed, bids should be secured from competent firms stating clearly what work is proposed and the cost involved. It may be discovered that the expense of repairs warrants replacement of the instrument. Careful records should be kept of all music instruments owned by the church, showing their location in the building, dates of purchase, tuning, and repairs. This should be done for all instruments, including those under service contracts. Names of those who have serviced the instruments should also be kept on file.

FURNITURE

A major responsibility of the maintenance staff is to keep the pews, chairs, tables, pianos and other furniture properly cleaned and in orderly arrangement. Discarded articles have a way of accumulating on the tops of pianos and tables and on the shelves of pulpits and lecterns. The maintenance supervisor should indicate to the cleaning personnel what is of continuing value and where these items should be stored. Other materials should be sent to their proper location or discarded.

Loose joints in chairs, tables, pews, and other furniture should be repaired. Neglect leads to breakage and possible injury. Most janitors can make simple repairs. Items that cannot be repaired by the maintenance staff should be called to the attention of the property managemnt committee for appropriate action.

COMMUNION AND BAPTISMAL EQUIPMENT

The communion service should be kept immaculately clean. Linens, trays, and glasses should be washed and stored in a dust proof and pest free location. Cracked or broken glasses should be discarded and replaced. Baptismal equipment should be kept in good condition. It should be clean and readily available for use.

ALL THINGS IN ORDER

Matching offering plates should be provided and kept well polished. They should be placed in their proper location preceding each worship service. Hymnbooks should be placed in the racks on the pews. Bindings should be repaired when needed. Obsolete bulletins, scraps of paper, and other extraneous items should be removed from pew racks and hymnbooks each week. Pictures and other aids to worship should be dusted and properly arranged.

AUTOMOBILES AND BUSES

The most frequently used pattern for providing transportation for the professional ministries of the pastor and other staff members is to include in the church budget an item for travel expense. This is usually a fixed amount paid along with the salary checks. Some churches provide oil-company credit cards and pay the actual expense incurred by operating the automobile, whether it is owned by the pastor or by the church. Some churches purchase or lease automobiles and, meeting all operating costs, furnish them to the pastor. These matters should be discussed by the pastor and the appropriate church committee at the beginning of his ministry. Changes may appropriately be considered at the time of planning the church budget. Maintenance of automobiles is exceedingly important if trouble-free service is to be expected.

Ownership of a bus places on the church the responsibility of keeping it in safe operating condition and seeing that it is always driven by competent drivers. Insurance coverage should be sufficient to cover damages from any and all injuries or fatalities that might occur. Demands for the use of the bus by church groups, and by some outside the church, will likely be great. Before a bus is purchased, definite policies regarding its use should be carefully considered and adopted. A designated official of the church should see that routine services are performed to keep the bus in good repair.

Since church buses operate on days and schedules not familiar to the motoring public, it is important that all safety precautions possible be taken in loading and unloading passengers. One helpful device that may be installed on buses is an amplifier with both interior and exterior loudspeakers. This enables the driver, remaining in his seat where he has better view of traffic, to call out directions and supervise those crossing roadways as they enter or leave the bus. Schools using such systems report better safety records.

Chapter Summary

1. New pianos need tuning three or four times during the first year and once or twice a year thereafter.

2. Contracts with reputable companies are advisable for the tuning and servicing of organs and pianos.

3. Automobiles and buses should be adequately insured and kept in excellent operating condition to provide safe travel and to protect against liability claims.

SAFETY MEASURES

THE PROPERTY MANAGEMENT committee and other custodians of church property are vitally concerned about prevention of accidents, fire, and disease. One of their chief responsibilities is to provide a safe place for people to assemble for worship, education, and service.

ACCIDENT PREVENTION

Accidents do occur, despite careful planning and diligent efforts to prevent them. The incidence of accidents seems to vary according to the age of the people involved. Preschool children have a higher accident rate than older children do. Older adults, sometimes limited in physical strength and coordination, must also be protected against accidents. There is need for great care in designing and arranging rooms to be used by younger children and older adults.

Drinking fountains and storage cabinets should be recessed into the walls to minimize them as a cause of accidents. Furniture should be rugged and tip proof. Halls and stairways should be well lighted. The surfaces of steps and ramps should be abrasive to prevent slipping and should be equipped with handrails.

External steps can present a serious hazard when

covered by ice or snow. Handrails should be kept in good condition and firmly anchored.

Serious hazards in many church buildings are the single steps that lead from one room to another or to a hallway. These are the spots where most falls occur. If possible, ramps should be installed to replace such steps where the difference in floor levels is not great.

FIRE PREVENTION

More than 4,000 fires annually do tremendous damage to church property in the United States. Fortunately, the death toll in church fires has not been high because most occur when the buildings are empty. Yet potential danger threatens during special occasions, such as Christmas pageants and other dramatic programs, when improvised lighting overloads circuits, when flammable stage settings and costumes are used, and when buildings are crowded. Property management committees and maintenance employees should insist on the use of approved electrical wiring. Flammable materials should be sprayed with flame-proof compounds. Aisles and exits should be kept open so that the building can be quickly and safely evacuated in case of fire.

Regular inspection of church buildings should include examination of fire extinguishers, heating facilities, electrical wiring, motors, appliances, sweeping and cleaning compounds, and storage areas.

Storage of flammable liquids, such as gasoline for power mowers, should receive special attention. Flammable material and equipment should be placed in fire-retardant areas, never in the furnace room. If the church uses a coal furnace, ashes should be placed in metal containers and removed as soon as possible. They should never be piled on the floor or placed in combustible containers for storage or removal. Old papers and all forms of combustible material should be removed from the church building.

Exit lights should be operating whenever the building is open. Stairways should be free of all obstructions. Fire escapes should be checked regularly to insure that they are usable.

SPRINKLER SYSTEMS

Church buildings in which fire hazard is a serious problem should have a sprinkler system. Such an arrangement involves installation of water pipes in or near the ceilings of all rooms, stairways, and halls. Sprinkler heads are attached to the water pipes at regular intervals. If heat rises to the danger point, thermostatic connections open the valves in the sprinkler heads and thus release water to extinguish the fire. When the building is unoccupied for extended periods of time, a sprinkler system can combat a fire that would otherwise make disastrous headway before discovery. Insurance companies offer favorable rates for sprinkler-equipped buildings.

FIRE-ALARM SYSTEMS

One of the simplest and most easily installed fire-alarm systems is a self-contained, self-powered unit with a thermostatic device that releases compressed gas to actuate an alarm mechanism. This type is suitable where people are near enough to hear and respond to an alarm. Other alarm systems involve electrically operated bells inside and outside the building. Connections may also relay the alarm to the nearest fire department. These systems have thermostatic devices in various parts of the building that throw the switch on the alarm mechanism when the temperature reaches the danger point at any one of the locations.

Maintenance personnel at the church, and fire-protection officials in the community, should regularly inspect and test all fire alarm, sprinkler, and extinguisher equipment so as to keep them in immediately usable condition.

Church members and staff personnel should be instructed to call the local fire department immediately when a fire is detected and to use available extinguishers to fight the fire until professional help arrives. The fire department telephone number should be prominently displayed near church telephones. If, however, the fire department uses alarm boxes to receive reports of fires, the location of the closest box should be indicated near the telephone and near each fire extinguisher.

INSULATION IS FIRE RETARDATION

One usually thinks of insulation as a means of reducing fuel consumption and preventing cold drafts. Insulation also helps reduce the need for interior painting by preventing "ghost streaks" on ceilings and walls at points of laths, studs, rafters, and joints. Another major contribution of insulation is that of providing a protective layer of fire retardant material in areas where fires may start and burn unnoticed until the entire structure is threatened. The furnace or boiler rooms should be enclosed with fire-resistant walls, ceilings, and floors. An approved fire door at the entrance, preferably an outside entrance, to the boiler room should be provided.

Chapter Summary

1. Good programs of property maintenance help prevent accidents and fires.

2. Churches should maintain fire extinguishers at points of greatest danger of fire and should teach their members and staff how to use them.

3. Fire detection and alarm systems are particularly needed in parts of church buildings that are not often used.

FOOD SERVICES

WHO SHOULD be responsible for administering food service? Most churches probably should delegate this work to a committee on food service. In some churches, much of the day-to-day work of the committee is done by a director of food service who plans menus, purchases food, and supervises the preparing and serving of meals by either paid or volunteer workers. The food-service committee, in consultation with the director of food service, should initiate policies and practices pertaining to this area of responsibility.

The committee on food service should see that the following items are provided and are readily available for inspection or review:

Policies and rules regarding the kitchen and its use
Job descriptions of food-service director and of kitchen help
Up-to-date inventory of food-service equipment and supplies and a description of present location and condition of such equipment
Manuals of instruction for operation of kitchen equipment
Requirements of Board of Health, also records of inspection and rating of this particular food-service facility

Health certificates and other pertinent information on employees

Record of costs of food, supplies, and labor

Recipes and menus

Summary report on each meal served

Calendar of occasions at which facilities will be used

ESSENTIAL FACTORS

Effective operation and maintenance of church food services requires systematic application of certain minimum essentials, which include:

1. Adequate provision for purchasing, receiving, and storing food and related supplies
2. Proper arrangement of physical facilities into efficient operating units for each step in the preparation of food
3. Proper provisions for serving food efficiently and in good condition
4. Dining area properly arranged and equipped
5. Adequate facilities for cleaning and storing china, glasses, silverware, trays, and related items
6. Necessary facilities for properly cleaning and storing pots and pans
7. Provisions for keeping food-service areas in a clean and sanitary condition
8. Proper and convenient provisions for garbage and trash disposal
9. Provision of physical facilities necessary for the convenience of the workers[1]

POLICIES AND RULES

Church-adopted policies should govern committee and staff decisions regarding who, when, how, and for what

[1] Adapted from Clarence Schroeder, *Church Food Service*, published by General Electric Company, Commercial Equipment Department, Chicago Heights, Illinois. Used by permission.

purposes food-service facilities may be used. A food-service calendar can be very helpful in implementing policies and in avoiding conflicts in scheduling.

The following illustration of rules and regulations may be a helpful guide to the use of church food-service facilities:

USE OF OUR FOOD-SERVICE FACILITIES[2]

1. Will be granted to any group of our church for fellowship meetings at times that will not conflict with regular or special worship services of the church, or with other meetings, or with activities which make it improper or inadvisable for the kitchen to be in use.

2. May be granted to responsible persons for wedding receptions at times that will not conflict with its use for fellowship meetings of the church organizations or with activities which make it inadvisable for the kitchen to be in use.

3. Must be arranged through the church office on a "first come—first served" basis. Use of the kitchen facilities by more than one group having simultaneous, separate meetings may be allowed if feasible and acceptable to all concerned. The kitchen will be kept locked except when in use by authorized persons or groups. Key may be obtained from the church office during office hours of the day of use and must be returned to the office immediately after its use. Key may be deposited in mail slot if office is closed.

4. May be denied to any group which fails to comply completely with these rules and regulations. It should be remembered that the purpose of these rules and regulations is not to make the use of the kitchen hard or unpleasant. Rather, it is to make it easier and more pleasant for all concerned. Each group is only one of dozens in our

[2] *Church Administration*, V, No. 3 (1963), 13-14.

church, and each one has the right to use our facilities. If all of us will be careful to observe these rules in the spirit of the Golden Rule, none will be disappointed.

5. Will require that all persons who use it will scrupulously observe the strictest rules of sanitation, cleanliness, and order—remembering that the next user has the right to find the room and all its equipment thoroughly clean and fresh and ready for use.

6. Specifically requires that:

a. All pots, pans, cutlery, dishes, and glasses shall be washed, dried, and returned to proper places of storage the same day they are used. In no case are dirty dishes or utensils to be left overnight.

b. No prepared foods are to be left in the kitchen after its use; they must be disposed of by those in charge. In rare cases, if necessary, such foods may be left in the refrigerator overnight, but must be promptly and properly disposed of the next day.

c. Any staple nonspoilable foodstuffs (such as sugar, salt, flour, seasonings) left in the kitchen become the property of the church and may be used by any church groups using the kitchen. Such items must be stored in covered containers provided for this purpose.

d. No garbage or trash of any kind shall be left in the kitchen overnight; it shall be placed in the cans provided, covered, and set outside the exterior kitchen door.

e. All cloths and towels used shall be thoroughly washed and spread out to dry on the towel bars provided.

f. After each use, the stove shall be wiped clean and any spilled grease, food, or liquids thoroughly removed.

g. The manufacturer's directions for use of the coffee urn (posted elsewhere in the kitchen) shall be carefully followed. After each use the urn and all its parts shall be thoroughly cleaned, rinsed, and left dry and open for ventilation.

h. All banquet tables shall be wiped clean and dry.

i. All counters, tabletops, shelves, and sinks in the kitchen shall be wiped clean and dry.

j. The dish cart shall be thoroughly washed, cleaned, and dried.

k. The kitchen floor shall be thoroughly swept after each use, with special attention and wet-mop cleaning given to any spots where food or grease has been spilled. (It should be remembered that grease will materially and permanently damage asphalt-tile flooring. Prompt and thorough cleaning should be done for any flooring soiled anywhere in the building.)

l. Any and all breakage of, or damage to, equipment or fixtures shall be reported in writing to the church office at the time of the return of the key.

m. It shall be the duty of any person observing same to report promptly to the church office the failure of any fixture or equipment to operate properly or any other matter needing adjustment or repair.

n. Paper tablecloth, provided by the church, is expected to be used only once. This material will be kept in the table-storage room. It is expected and required that whenever any person opens the last full roll, he will notify the church office promptly so that additional material may be ordered.

FOOD-SERVICE PERSONNEL

All salaried staff personnel involved in food preparation or service, or in dishwashing, should be employed by the director of food service in consultation with the food-service committee and in accord with personnel policies established by the church. Procedures of employing food-service staff should be in keeping with those used in employing other members of the church staff.

FOOD-SERVICE AREAS

Food-service areas must be kept clean. Failure to do so would increase the possibility of food poisoning and resultant unhappy public relations. Civil jurisdictions have rigid health regulations for protection of people to whom food service is rendered. Churches should make sure to observe all health regulations and the highest standards of health protection. Construction or remodeling of kitchens should be done only in consultation with state or local health authorities.

The size of the church and the frequency of use of food-service facilities should, of course, be considered in determining adequacy of equipment for food service. But regardless of size, and no matter whether the food-service facilities are used once a month or every day, the highest standards of cleanliness should prevail.

Design of food-service facilities should be determined by the use intended and the kind of help available. The arrangement should be sufficiently flexible to permit either cafeteria service or serving of plates in the dining room. Church kitchens should be spacious enough for a large number of workers, since several volunteers are usually involved rather than a few professional cooks. Counter space, for filling plates, and serving carts should be available when tables are served by workers. There should be adequate storage space for all kitchen utensils, china, and silverware. Since most dining areas are used for other purposes, there should be adequate and convenient storage space for dining tables not in use. To avoid a noise problem, the dishwashing area should be located as far from the dining area as possible, preferably in a separate room adjoining the main kitchen.

KITCHEN EQUIPMENT

The kitchen should be equipped with locked cabinets for storing equipment and supplies. Adequate refrigerators and freezers greatly facilitate good food storage and permit advance preparation of many items on the menu. Institutional or commercial equipment for use in church kitchens is preferable to residential equipment. A carbon-dioxide or dry-chemical fire extinguisher for use against grease fires and electrical fires should be available in the kitchen. Doors and serving windows connecting kitchen and dining area should be closable to reduce kitchen noise in dining area when meetings are in progress there.

Kitchen walls, floors, and equipment should be constructed to minimize health hazards. Walls are more easily cleaned if they are of enameled plaster or ceramic tile, or are covered with plastic. Ceilings should be of enameled plaster or plastic finish. Used in kitchen areas, acoustical tile absorbs grease and collects dirt, reducing its acoustical properties. Moreover, acoustical tile is not easily cleaned.

Floors may be covered with grease-proof vinyl, asphalt, or rubber tile. Quarry tile and ceramic tile are easily cleaned and are quite serviceable but are not as comfortable for workers spending hours in the kitchen. Wood floors are not desirable because they are difficult to keep clean. Concrete is not comfortable underfoot and, because it is porous, is not easy to keep clean.

Large windows with frosted glass are recommended. An exhaust fan should provide forced ventilation. A hood over the cooking area, with a grease interceptor in the exhaust fan duct work, will keep kitchen odors from circulating throughout the remainder of the building. Grease should not be permitted to accumulate on the range, range hood, exhaust fan, grease ducts, or walls.

Kitchen equipment should be chosen for its durability, usefulness, and ease of cleaning and maintenance. Rolled-edge, stainless-steel counter tops and tabletops are desirable. Besides being quickly and easily cleaned, they resist corrosion and staining. Legs and joints should be secured with flush, streamlined fittings to avoid unnecessary cracks, crevices, bolt heads, and other dirt-catching areas. Adequate storage of items in a location that is as close as possible to their point of use greatly reduces traffic and saves time and energy. Commercial-size pots and pans and professional cutlery, rather than ordinary household types, ensure better work with less effort and are more durable.

GARBAGE DISPOSAL

Since garbage draws roaches, rats, mice, and flies, it should be removed from the food-service area as quickly as possible. Local conditions and available equipment will determine how best to dispose of accumulated garbage. The ideal means of removal of most food waste, such as peelings, is a garbage disposal unit installed in the plumbing system. This chops garbage into small pieces that are washed into the sewer line. However, a good many churches find an automatic incinerator their best solution, though this requires that garbage and other waste material be wrapped in small bundles before being placed into the incinerator.

Chapter Summary

1. Church food service should provide wholesome meals prepared and served under sanitary conditions at modest cost.

2. The committee on food service should recommend and observe policies and rules regarding the use and maintenance of food-service facilities.

3. The kitchen should be thoroughly cleaned immediately after the preparation and serving of each meal.

4. Commercial kitchen equipment, preferably of stainless steel, is recommended for use in churches.

CHURCH GROUNDS

PROPER USE of land surrounding a church building can help make the church an attractive and appreciated
neighbor whether in city, town, or country. Fortunate is
the church that has adequate land for the many activities
needing space adjacent to or near the church buildings.

Well-landscaped grounds help mold the building and
land into a complete unit. By passing through a beautifully landscaped entrance, people approaching the place
of worship can be refreshed and prepared psychologically
for the experience awaiting them.

LANDSCAPING

A beautiful and well-constructed church building
can lose much of its esthetic and symbolic beauty if it
is set in a poorly landscaped environment. The church
that has a master plan for development of its real estate
and that has given adequate attention to the external
appearance of its building and surrounding grounds has
been well advised. A competent landscape architect should
be consulted in the making of such over-all plans.

Through effective landscaping, existing church buildings can be greatly improved in over-all beauty, attractiveness, and symbolic communication. A careful study

should be made of the plot plan, the topography, and the need for parking areas, driveways, and walks. Consideration should be given also to the most effective arrangement of trees, shrubbery, and flowers. A building is not truly finished until it is properly landscaped.

The property management committee, assisted by competent counsel, should recommend plans for landscaping the church grounds, including parking lots. This committee should also determine the best arrangement for off-street parking.

MAINTAINING THE GROUNDS

The property management committee and the maintenance staff should have as their objective the maintenance of the grounds surrounding the church in a clean and orderly manner. The general appearance of the building and its surroundings should be inviting and reflect the love and care which the members have for their place of worship. A well cared for building, even if not expensive, can be quite impressive when surrounded by well-landscaped grounds. The lawn should be well sodded, free of weeds, and carefully mowed.

Proper maintenance protects the health, safety, and convenience of those who use the church property. Maintenance of grounds and walks should facilitate keeping the building clean inside and reduce noises that would interfere with programs of the church.

MAINTENANCE STANDARDS

The property management committee should carefully determine the maintenance needs of the church property and the specific duties and responsibilities of maintenance personnel. If the parsonage and other church-owned dwellings are to be cared for by the church maintenance staff, this responsibility should be specified in the work schedule of such employees.

Walks should be kept free of debris and other obstructions. Convenient trash containers, painted green to blend with adjacent shrubs, should be placed near walks. Fences, if any, should be kept in good repair and attractively painted.

Fixed and movable signs should be maintained in attractive condition. Keep lettering legible and attractive. Replace burned-out or broken light bulbs. Local laws governing size and location of signs should be observed.

A maintenance plan that includes a blueprint or other graphic presentation of the church grounds should specify location of trees, shrubs, flowers, grass areas, signs, driveways, walks, and parking areas.

CHOOSING PLANTS

A competent landscape architect or nurseryman can help choose plants that look well together and are suited to the building or lawn area where they are placed. Shrubs and trees should be grouped to provide an attractive frame for viewing buildings and grounds. They may be used to screen parking areas, to set off church property from adjacent residential or commercial areas, or to serve as a partial barrier to traffic noise from nearby streets or highways.

Hardy, slow-growing shrubs that require little maintenance are preferable for church grounds. They should be selected with their mature height and spread in mind. In a bed or foundation planting, tallest varieties should be planted to the rear, medium- and low-growing shrubs in front. Consult a reliable garden manual for recommended pruning time.

Maintenance personnel should be provided with instruction sheets specifying what spraying, fertilizing, trimming, and cultivating is needed for trees and shrubs. Specific instructions should also be given for weed removal, watering, and mowing. A list of grounds-maintenance equipment provided by the church, with instructions for its use, upkeep, and storage, should be available to maintenance personnel.

TRAINING EMPLOYEES IN GROUNDS CARE

The property management committee should not assume that maintenance personnel know how to provide adequate care for church grounds. To avoid personal injury, employees should be instructed in the operation of power equipment. Proper training of employees usually fosters better work, resulting in more attractive grounds.

LAWN CARE

An attractive lawn requires properly prepared soil and fertilization as required by soil conditions. It may be necessary to add organic matter to sandy soils or clay, in order to provide better conditions for plant growth. Peat moss or compost can supply needed organic matter. Establishing or reworking grass areas may require removal of debris left from construction and the addition of sufficient topsoil for plant growth. Good drainage is essential for root growth, and the ground should be properly leveled to guarantee adequate drainage before grass seed is planted.

Use of Power Equipment: A church with an extensive lawn usually owns power mowers and edgers. Operators should know and observe rules for safe operation of such equipment. Machines should be in good working order, blades securely fastened, safety guards in place, and all nuts and bolts tight. Before starting the machine, go over the lawn to remove all foreign objects. Stand behind the machine when starting the motor, and do not leave the motor running without a hand on the controls. When the blade is turning, do not try to pick up foreign objects immediately in the path of the machine.

Before starting the machine, check to see that the oil

in the crankcase is at the proper level, that the air filter is functioning properly, that the air screen is clean, and that the grease fittings, oil cups, and gasoline tank are filled.

TREE CARE

One aspect of grounds care frequently neglected is the proper care of trees. Edgar D. Dunning[1] says "a neglected roof soon develops a leak and demands attention; a neglected lawn soon advertises its distress with browned and weedy areas, but a neglected tree stands patiently and suffers with little outward sign of its desperate need, often until it is beyond saving." Trees need loose, well-treated soil, but in the effort to keep an attractive growth of grass on the lawn, the soil may be kept free of any mulch and is often packed tight by foot traffic and lawn mowers. Fertilizer applied only on the surface is used up by the grass before it reaches the deeper tree roots. The areas from which trees can draw sustenance are often restricted by walks, driveways, parkings areas, and building foundations.

Dunning recommends a generous annual feeding of all trees with "a mixture of super-phosphate and dried, ground cow manure. . . . The phosphates are available immediately to the trees; the manure gives up its nitrogen and other chemicals more slowly throughout the growing season.

"The amount needed can be determined by a commonly used formula. To the height of the tree in feet, add the diameter of its crown in feet and the circumference of its trunk in inches, and apply that number of pounds of mixed fertilizer. For example, a tree 50 feet high and 40 feet in crown diameter and 100 inches in trunk circumference at breast height should have 50 plus 40 plus

[1] Edgar D. Dunning, "Care of Campus Trees Shouldn't Be Left to Nature," *College and University Business*, XXXVI, No. 4 (1964), 66. Used by permission.

100, or a total of 190 pounds of fertilizer each year, preferably applied early in the growing season. Application is simple. Make a circle of shallow holes about 18 inches deep and 18 inches apart and in each hole drop a generous measure of fertilizer.

"Pruning is important," says Dunning, "not only because it makes the tree more sightly, but also because it removes deadwood which harbors grubs and insects that spread disease and encourage decay. . . . Pruning can be done at any time of year, but the scars heal more quickly if it is done at the end of the dormant period or the beginning of the growing period, i.e. from late March to mid-May. It is common practice to paint all raw ends more than two inches in diameter with asphaltum or orange shellac. . . . Cutting should be done with a saw or with clippers, but never with an ax or a hatchet."

In addition to feeding and pruning, trees should be sprayed to kill leaf-eating insects and other pests. Local conditions, including the practice of owners of other trees in the neighborhood, determine how often spraying is needed.

LOCATING AND CONSTRUCTING WALKS

Walks should enhance the beauty of buildings and grounds, leaving space for landscape plantings where needed. Paved areas around major entrances should be large enough for groups to gather without trampling shrubbery, flowers, or lawns.

Walks should be constructed of materials that are not easily tracked into the buildings. Grass and shrubs along walks should be trimmed so as not to brush against the passersby.

FLOODLIGHTING

Floodlighting can enhance church buildings. Lights may feature a tower, a steeple, an entrance, a landscaped area, or a stained-glass window. Floodlighting identifies and advertises the building as a church. Safety and security provided to church premises and to those who use them are especially good reasons for having well-lighted buildings and grounds.

PARKING FACILITIES

Adequate, well-located, and properly constructed parking areas can augment a church's drawing power.

Maintaining an attractive parking area can create goodwill in the neighborhood. In some cities, church members practically monopolize all street parking space at certain times. Because of this problem, some cities require new churches to provide parking space in direct ratio to the number of people expected to occupy the building on usual occasions.

Parking areas that are dusty, muddy, or poorly maintained may cause complaints from neighbors. Good public relations with members who use the parking area and with neighbors who see it every day indicate the wisdom of properly locating, maintaining, and landscaping it. The harsh barrenness of many parking areas can be relieved by use of properly arranged screen planting.

The entrance to church parking lots should be accessible, well marked, and attractive. Angled parking on either side of the one-way drives produces less congestion. Curving drives or angles are more easily beautified than straightaways. They also discourage speeding. Parking lots with one-way traffic usually operate more smoothly.

Attractive and convenient parking space is extremely important. Designs calling for parking at 45- or 60-degree angles off a one-way drive are increasingly popular. Parking-lot entrances and exits should be located in consideration of maximum pedestrian safety, minimum traffic congestion, and maximum convenience of major entrances to church buildings.

Suggestions in the church paper and on bulletin boards can inform the congregation regarding preferred areas for unloading and use of walks for pedestrian traffic. Volunteer or paid workers may be needed to direct incoming cars to available parking space.

SAFETY FACTORS IN PARKING

Most people come to church by automobile. In many cases, passengers are unloaded in areas where traffic is heavy. Children are often let out near the entrance to the building, and the driver drives on to find a parking place. Impulsive children will be tempted to cross the street in the midst of heavy traffic. Such problems may be avoided by locating loading and unloading areas off the driveways. Parking areas should be designed so that passengers will not need to cross the line of automobile traffic to enter the building.

SURFACING PARKING AREAS

Materials most commonly used for parking areas are crushed stone, blacktop, or concrete. Although the initial cost of concrete may be considerably higher, long-range average costs per year may be less where extreme weather conditions may cause deterioration of other materials. Care should be taken to keep down dust that may be blown or tracked into the church building.

COMMERCIAL USE
OF CHURCH PARKING AREAS

Many churches in or near commercial districts arrange with neighboring businesses to share the cost and the use of parking space. Others lease commercial parking lots or parking garage space. A few churches own parking buildings that are available free to church members for all church activities. These may also be operated commercially, with income retiring the cost of providing the parking facility.

Churches considering a commercial-type parking building should be certain to consult experts in the parking business for advice on designs and building standards. Labor costs are considerably reduced by following a self-parking system. Sixty-degree angle parking from one-way drives is advisable where feasible. Drivers find it easier to use angle-parking spaces without blocking flow of incoming and outgoing traffic.

MAINTENANCE AND CLEANING OF PARKING AREAS

Commercial sweeper companies that contract with shopping centers and other parking lot owners to sweep their parking lots are available in some cities. Such a contract might save the church from purchasing expensive equipment which would be used infrequently.

Painted lines on an unobstructed surface simplify cleaning, and in areas where snow must be removed, are preferable to curbs or dividers for marking parking areas. Double stripes, one foot apart, encourage drivers to center their cars without overcrowding and thus provide room to leave and enter each car. Special paints are available for this purpose. A space nine feet by nineteen feet should be provided for each car. If the parking area is also to be used for recreation, lines marking off playing courts should be painted yellow: parking lanes and stalls should be white.

OUTDOOR RECREATION FACILITIES

Where space is available, churches may provide for many forms of outdoor recreation. Paved areas can double as basketball, badminton, and volleyball courts. Shuffleboard courts and facilities for horseshoes and similar games can be provided even where space is quite limited. Some churches have baseball and softball fields. Many have space for playground equipment such as swings, slides, and climbing devices. Such equipment must be solidly installed and carefully maintained to avoid accidents.

OUTDOOR WORSHIP AREAS

In communities where weather conditions are favorable, churches have found outdoor worship areas an attractive addition to their facilities. In some cases they are established adjacent to parking areas for use as "drive-in" worship centers. If movable folding chairs are brought from the buildings for occasional use outdoors, terraces from three to four feet wide should be graded into the sloping area to provide level space for rows of chairs. Shrubs may be used to screen off the area from noise and the lights of passing automobiles. Shrubs and trees can be used to form a backdrop for the platform area.

Chapter Summary

1. Good landscaping enhances the beauty, attractiveness, and symbolic communication of church buildings.

2. Adequate parking facilities, conveniently located, attract and retain church members.

Chapter 14

PARSONAGES

THE HAPPINESS of the pastor's family and his over-all effectiveness are of vital concern to every congregation. Few things are more influential in determining the satisfaction of the pastor and his family than the condition of the house in which they live. Any survey of pastors' wives would quickly reveal the usually undisclosed unhappiness, and sometimes actual physical suffering, resulting from inadequately constructed and poorly maintained houses that churches provide for them. In these days when business and industry seek suitable means of providing their valuable executives with attractive fringe benefits, churches may well reexamine their provision of dwellings for their pastors.

Maintaining an attractive residence for the pastor is an important factor in attracting and holding adequate ministerial leadership. Time and funds placed in parsonage improvements are good investments. Certainly the pastor's satisfaction and tenure are enhanced by providing his family an attractive, comfortable home with modern equipment.

THE QUESTION OF OWNERSHIP

Traditionally, most churches have provided church-owned dwellings for their pastors. Now, a good many churches provide a housing allowance for their pastors, giving them the choice of obtaining the kind of housing facilities they prefer in the area of the community in which they wish to live. The question of which arrangement is best may well be answered locally, probably in relation to availability of suitable housing at the time the pastor needs it. On the other hand, church-owned dwellings may not be easily adaptable to the varying needs of successive occupants. A childless couple or a bachelor may be followed by a family with six children. Some pastors wish to live in proximity to other property of the church. Others prefer to be at considerable distance in order to provide a measure of privacy for themselves and their families.

If the church does choose to own and operate a dwelling for its pastor, or other staff members, then it should accept full responsibility for keeping the house in excellent condition.

MULTIPLE USE OF PARSONAGE

Generally, pastors wish their home to provide a place of privacy and relaxation. Many however prefer to have a study in their home and ask those coming for counseling to meet them there. Some pastors wish to have committees and other church groups meet at the parsonage to provide a more informal atmosphere. Practice in this regard should be determined by the desires of the pastor and his family.

CHOOSING THE LOCATION

Should the parsonage be adjacent to the church premises, or should it be some distance away? This is a vital question for clergymen and for churches.

Some reasons for having the parsonage adjacent to other property of the church, according to Elbert M. Conover,[1] are:

[1] Elbert M. Conover, *The Parsonage, Planning and Building It,* Department of Church Building, National Council of Churches, 475 Riverside Drive, New York, N.Y., copyright 1951, p. 7. Used with permission.

1. The pastor's home is more easily recognized as a part of the religious establishment.
2. There is more effective impact upon the community by the total church institution.
3. There are likely to be more contacts with the church people and therefore a greater number of opportunities for personal service to the people.
4. The home is protected at least on one side of the parsonage property from noisy or uncongenial neighbors.
5. The members of the parsonage family do not need to be transported to the several church services and meetings. The pastor does not have to feel responsible for transporting the members of his family who may need to go to the church at different times.
6. The pastor may appreciate the opportunity of retiring to his home for a few minutes of seclusion between meetings, such as between Sunday School and the worship service.
7. Church officials are more likely to give needed consideration to the upkeep and care of the parsonage if it is adjacent to the church building.
8. In some places, if the pastor's home is recognized as a part of the church establishment, taxation on the home is thereby avoided.

Many pastors, particularly those with young children, insist that when the home is away from the church the family is able to live a more normal life. Sometimes a compelling reason for locating the parsonage away from the church is that land near the church building is urgently needed for other buildings or for parking.

A pastor should usually live in the area in which most of his people live. The man who would preach to the city should be willing to live in the city. To reach those in rural or small-town communities, he should live among them.

REMODEL OR RELOCATE?

How much money should be spent on bringing a church-owned dwelling up to acceptable standards? A prior question might be whether this is a comfortable and suitable home for our pastor. Because someone bequeathed a house to the church years ago need not mean that the church should not provide modern and appropriate housing for the present day.

New layers of paint or wallpaper will not do much for a house with 14-foot ceilings, drafty windows and doors, cold floors, and long stairways. If such old houses must be used, the high ceilings should be lowered by using attractive insulating materials. Doors can be weather-stripped, windows caulked, walls and ceilings insulated, and adequate heating and cooling systems installed. Wall-to-wall carpeting can add comfort and beauty to old floors.

Modernizing an old house, however, can be very expensive. Old fireplaces can be disguised, covered, or left open to further increase the heating bill. Inadequate wiring with extension cords running everywhere can endanger the lives of the family.

The cost of satisfactory remodeling plus recurring expense of upkeep and high heating bills often indicate that it would be wise to sell the old house and obtain one that is modern and appropriately arranged.

SURVEYING THE DWELLING

The procedures already outlined for a careful survey of other church buildings should be followed in examining the condition of the present parsonage or of any dwelling being considered for purchase. Churches needing to decide whether to buy a parsonage or build one should carefully consider the latter in order to provide any unique features that may be needed.

The initial survey of the dwelling should be followed by

frequent inspections made by the property management committee. A checklist that includes the following items should be used:

1. Exterior paint, wood finishes, masonry
2. Roofing, walls, basements
3. Floors, windows and doors, weatherproofing
4. Interior paint and other wall surfacing
5. Utility systems—heating, cooling, plumbing, electricity
6. Lawns, shrubs, trees, fencing, walks, driveways

EQUIPPING THE PASTOR'S HOME

Some churches provide not only a parsonage but also some or all of the furniture, floor coverings, curtains, and drapes. Where this practice prevails, the church should keep these items in attractive and usable condition. Installation of a permanent television antenna suitable for the area is also advisable. Landscaping, permanent planting, and if needed, an enclosed play area should be provided by the church.

LAWN CARE

Who should take care of the parsonage lawn? Some pastors prefer to assign this task to the church sexton. Others enjoy doing this work themselves. Agreement on this matter should be reached at the time a new pastor comes to the church. If considerable time and effort are needed for care of the parsonage lawn, the church should make provision for such care, to permit the pastor to give his time to more pressing needs of the church.

Suggestions in Chapter 13 regarding landscaping and lawn care are applicable also to the parsonage.

USING VOLUNTEER HELP

In the maintenance and improvement of the pastor's home, the volunteer labor of the church members sometimes may be used to good advantage. The men of the church often can be enlisted for such work. They can paint, insulate, weatherstrip, re-roof, landscape, and otherwise aid in making the pastor's home comfortable, attractive, and adequate.

Chapter Summary

1. Churches should provide for their pastors either adequate housing allowances or modern and comfortable church-owned dwellings.

2. Church-owned dwellings should be kept in excellent condition. If the present parsonage is unsuitable or needs costly remodeling, the church probably should purchase a new dwelling, preferably some distance from the other property of the church.

Chapter 15

QUESTIONS FOR REVIEW AND DISCUSSION

*by Hugh G. E. Paull**

THE FOLLOWING QUESTIONS are intended to serve as a guide to further study of Dean Allen W. Graves' book on using and maintaining church real estate and equipment in accordance with effective standards of religious stewardship. They are based on and adapted from the syllabus of a course offered by the Center for Church Business Management, The American University, Washington, D.C., and are used in Dean Graves' book by special permission.

Some of the questions have been modified or rearranged to relate them better to the text. A few are answered, at least partially, in the Editor's Introduction. Others suggest ideas that were not intended to be treated explicitly in this book. Diligent search for valid answers to these questions should lead to a deeper appreciation of the process of managing church property within a context of predetermined religious purposes, objectives, and goals.

* Business Manager, First Baptist Church, Washington, D.C.; member of the Part-time Faculty, School of Business Adimimistration, The American University.

A. *Using Church Property*

1. In what significant respects should a church's approach to the use of its property differ from that of (a) other nonprofit charitable organizations, (b) commercial establishments, (c) government agencies? In what significant respects should the approach be either similar or identical?

2. In what ways should a church's approach to the use of its property be determined by (a) its voluntary nature, (b) its trustee relationship? In what respects should these two characteristics (a and b) make no particular difference?

3. Select two churches (preferably of two denominations) and obtain from each a copy of a published description of how it develops and promotes: (a) congregational concepts of its objectives and goals; (b) comprehensive programs that are generally understood and voluntarily accepted. What conclusions do you draw from this experience?

4. What is the difference between the two concepts in each of the following pairs: (a) policy and rule, (b) process and procedure, (c) purpose and function, (d) objective and goal, (e) forecast and plan, (f) program and project?

5. What are the responsibilities and duties of the chief governing body of your church? Which of the following words best describe its task: policy, procedure, process, program, plan? Should its role be primarily that of "a body of final deliberation"? Why, or why not?

6. Who in your church determines policy regarding use of buildings, grounds, and equipment? By what process or procedure is such policy formulated? Who is in charge of implementing the policy? What improvements in this practice would you recommend?

7. Under what conditions, or in what kinds of situations, might custodial personnel appropriately participate in formulating, implementing, or interpreting church policy regarding use of real estate and equipment?

8. By means of what programs does your church endeavor to accomplish its distinctive purposes, objectives, and goals? Do the physical facilities of your church meet the needs of its programs? Give reasons for your answer.

9. What established policies of your church govern the use of its property for activities not directly related to the church's avowed purposes, objectives, and goals? List several nonchurch organizations that used your church's property during the last year, specifying the areas or rooms and equipment they used.

10. By what procedures does your church determine whether its programming contributes to achievement of its distinctive purposes, objectives, and goals? Who makes the evaluation? How often are the goals systematically reviewed to determine their relevance and validity?

11. What changes are taking place in the vicinity of your church which may affect the character of its ministry with respect to (a) kinds of people to be served—age, education, economic status, culture, occupations, transiency; (b) mode of transportation—walking, public transit, private automobile using congested streets, rural roads or superhighways; (c) development of real estate in the area—single-family dwellings, high-rise or terrace apartments, industrial, commercial, government buildings? What is your church doing about it? What should it do?

12. What agencies in your community, and elsewhere, are available to help your church plan its programs to meet projected needs of its constituency ten years hence?

13. What changes should be made in your church's property to meet immediate needs for expansion or supplementation? What is the order of their urgency or importance? How would these changes, if made now, affect present plans for future needs?
14. What kind of inventory of your church's property (space and equipment) would you recommend? What records should be available? Where and how should they be preserved?
15. Comparing immediate program needs with the inventory of church property, what steps can be taken to use present space and equipment more effectively? How soon can this be done?
16. Following a comprehensive survey of program needs and available facilities, what controls will assure compliance with policies regarding use of church property?
17. Who schedules activities in your church and who assigns the space and equipment to be used? What policies guide these decisions? What procedure is followed in scheduling activities?
18. What significant developments or trends in the use of church property do you predict or suggest for the decade immediately ahead?

B. *Maintaining Church Property*

19. What distinguishes churches from other organizations (business, government, hospitals, schools) in their approach to the use and upkeep of their property? How do these differences affect custodial staffing with respect to enlistment, remuneration, morale, training, productivity, and efficiency?
20. Who in your church determines policy for maintenance of buildings, grounds, and equipment? By what means is such policy established? Who implements the policy? What improvements in this practice would you suggest?

21. Describe the property-maintenance program of your church, showing what is done by volunteers and what is done by employed staff. What improvements would you suggest?

22. Suggest three categories of property-maintenance work that may form a convenient and logical basis for organizing the maintenance staff. Under which category would each of the following be placed: (a) repairing the roof, (b) mowing the lawn, (c) operating a movie projector?

23. By what procedures may a church assure itself that its property is usable, clean, in good repair, in operating condition, and available when needed? Evaluate the saying that maintenance personnel will come nearer doing what's *in*spected than what's *ex*pected.

24. What kinds of custodial work schedules should be established? How can the schedules be enforced? Who may authorize departures from schedules?

25. What conditions might justify entering into a service contract for the maintenance of church equipment? What service is usually covered by a "full maintenance" contract for office equipment? Describe some other kinds of common service contracts for each of the following: (a) an air-conditioning system, (b) an industrial vacuum cleaner, (c) a permanently installed dishwasher.

26. What kinds of maintenance work can appropriately be performed by volunteers? What kinds of maintenance work should be done by paid custodians? What work should be contracted? What licenses are required for maintenance workers in your community?

27. What special-purpose equipment, instruments, and furnishings in a church ordinarily require special maintenance?

28. What security measures are necessary to protect church property from theft, fire, misplacement, or

other abuse? Who should have keys? How can a
church be kept secure while remaining open to all
who may need its ministries?

29. What standards can be used to determine whether
maintenance costs are within reasonable limits? How
much should a church spend for "housekeeping"?
What reserves for emergencies in property maintenance should be included in the church's annual
budget?

30. What are the advantages and disadvantages of carpeting as compared with asphalt tile or other surfaces
in connection with the maintenance of church floors?

31. What is meant by preventive maintenance? Describe
a preventive-maintenance program now being followed in your church.

REFERENCES

Books

Conover, H. S., *Grounds Maintenance Handbook* (2nd ed.). New York: F. W. Dodge Corporation, 1958.

Finchum, R. N., *Administering the Custodial Program.* Washington, D.C.: U.S. Government Printing Office, 1961.

Kotschevar, L. H. and Terrell, Margaret E., *Food Service Planning Layout and Equipment.* New York: John Wiley & Sons, Inc., 1961.

McClinton, Katharine M., *The Changing Church, It's Architecture, Art and Decoration.* New York: Morehouse-Gorman Company, 1957.

Murphy, Bonneau P., *The Building and Care of Methodist Church Property.* New York: Division of National Missions Board of Missions, The Methodist Church, 1961.

Roe, William H., *School Business Management.* New York: McGraw-Hill Book Company, Inc., 1961.

Scotford, John R., *How to Decorate Your Church.* Westwood, New Jersey: Fleming H. Revell Co., 1962.

Stiles, Joseph, *Acquiring and Developing Church Real Estate.* Englewood Cliffs, New Jersey: Prentice-Hall, Inc., 1965.

Taylor, Robert C., *How to Maintain Your Church Buildings*

and Grounds. Westwood, New Jersey: Fleming H. Revell Co., 1962.

Magazines

Buildings, The Magazine of Building Management, published monthly by Stamats Publishing Company, 427 Sixth Avenue, S.E., Cedar Rapids, Iowa.

Church Administration, published monthly by the Sunday School Board, Southern Baptist Convention, 127 Ninth Avenue, North, Nashville, Tennessee.

Church Management, published monthly by Church Management, Inc., 13308 Euclid Avenue, Cleveland, Ohio.

Institutions, published by Domestic Engineering Company, 1801 Prairie Avenue, Chicago, Illinois.

Modern Sanitation and Building Maintenance, published monthly by Powell Magazines, Inc., 855 Avenue of the Americas, New York, New York.

National Custodian, published by the American Institute of Maintenance, P.O. Box 2068, Glendale, California.

The Nation's Schools, published monthly by McGraw-Hill Book Company, Inc., 1050 Merchandise Mart, Chicago, Illinois.

Parking, National Parking Association, 711 Fourteenth Street, N.W., Washington, D.C.

Protestant Church Buildings and Equipment, published quarterly by the Christian Herald Publishing Company, 27 East 39th Street, New York, N.Y.

Your Church, Its Building-Equipment-Administration-Finances, published quarterly by the Religious Publishing Company, 122 Old York Road, Jenkintown, Pennsylvania.

Visual Aids

The Institute of Sanitation Management, 55 West 42nd Street, New York, N.Y. issues a list of visual aids for sanitation training. List indicates whether item is film or film strip, source, running time, and date.

Index

INDEX

Service contract, maintenance, 89
Service contract, musical instruments, 140-141
Service contract, office equipment, 89
Sexton, 53
Sick leaves, 57
Size of maintenance staff, 45
Sound-amplification systems, 132
Sprinkler systems, 146
Stainless steel, 100
Stripping waxed floor, 110-111
Supervision, 42, 59, 68-74
Supplies, 76

T

Taxes, 17-20
Tax exemption, 18
Terrazzo floors, 115
Testing, 66
Tile, asphalt, vinyl, rubber, 109

Tile, ceramic, 114
Title, legal, 20
Tools, 58
Training custodial staff, 62-66
Tree care, 160-161

V

Vacations, 57
Vandalism, 34-35
Volunteer labor, 44, 125, 170

W

Walks, 161
Walls, cleaning, 101
Washing, light fixtures, 97-98
Washing, walls, 101-102
Washing, windows, 98-99
Waterproofing, walls, 127-128
Weddings, 26-28
Work schedules, 59-61
Work standards, 43, 70
Worship, 15
Worship, outdoor, 165